DeFi vs TradFi

Pension Funds and Family Offices Embracing the Decentralized Finance Movement

By: *John E. Cornish III*

ISBN: 9798326843838

Foreword:

This book provides a comprehensive roadmap for exploring the journey of pension funds and family offices as they navigate the complex yet promising world of cryptocurrency investments.

In recent years, we've witnessed a profound shift in the investment landscape, as institutional investors increasingly recognize the transformative potential of cryptocurrency. Once viewed as a speculative asset on the fringes of finance,

cryptocurrency has now
emerged as a legitimate
investment option for
institutions seeking to
diversify their portfolios,
hedge against inflation, and
tap into the disruptive power
of blockchain technology.

One of the most compelling
trends driving institutional
adoption of cryptocurrency is
its role in securing workforce
retirement plans. As
traditional pension funds and
retirement schemes grapple
with low interest rates, volatile
markets, and mounting
pension liabilities, institutional
investors are turning to crypto

assets as a potential solution to safeguard retirement savings and ensure long-term financial stability for their workforce.

In this forward-looking environment, we invite you to explore the trend of institutional investors switching to crypto to secure their workforce retirement plans. Through insightful analysis, real-world case studies, and expert perspectives, we'll examine the motivations driving this trend, the challenges, and opportunities it presents, and the implications for the future of retirement planning and wealth management.

Join us on this journey as we delve into the intersection of cryptocurrency and institutional investing, exploring how digital assets are reshaping the retirement landscape and empowering institutions to navigate an uncertain economic future with confidence and foresight.

DeFi vs TradFi

Contents

Chapter 1: Pension Funds 8

Chapter 2: The Genesis 44

Chapter 3: The Early Adopters 89

Chapter 4: Crypto Landscape 111

Chapter 5: Institutional Investors .. 155

Chapter 6: Minting Our Own 179

Chapter 7: The Rising Tide 203

Chapter 8: Institutional Interest 234

Chapter 9: Why Institutions 284

Chapter 10: The Next Frontier 328

Chapter 11: The Revolution 342

Bonus Recap: 355

Chapter 1: Pension Funds

The adoption of cryptocurrency investments by pension funds and family offices marks a significant milestone in the financial industry. This chapter explores how these large institutional investors have increasingly embraced digital assets, highlighting their motivations, strategies, and the impact on the broader cryptocurrency market. We will delve into case studies, the evolving investment landscape, and the prospects of cryptocurrency investments for pension funds and family offices.

Pension funds and family offices were initially skeptical about investing in cryptocurrencies due to concerns about volatility, regulatory uncertainty, and the nascent nature of the market. However, as the industry matured, these institutions began to recognize the potential benefits of digital assets.

In the early years, cryptocurrencies were often associated with high-risk investments, largely driven by the speculative nature of the market and the frequent headlines about hacks and scams. Pension funds and family offices, known for their conservative investment strategies and fiduciary responsibilities, were understandably cautious.

One of the significant turning points was the gradual establishment of clearer regulatory frameworks.

Governments and financial authorities worldwide began to develop guidelines and regulations for cryptocurrencies, providing a more secure and predictable environment for institutional investors.

Another factor was the maturation of the cryptocurrency market. This played a critical role. As the market stabilized and the infrastructure improved, with better custodial services, trading platforms, and compliance tools, institutional investors started to see cryptocurrencies as a viable asset class.

The potential for diversification was another compelling reason for considering cryptocurrency investments. Cryptocurrencies, with their low correlation to traditional assets like stocks and bonds, offered pension funds and family offices a way to diversify their portfolios and potentially enhance returns while managing risk. Several key factors have driven pension funds and family offices to incorporate cryptocurrencies into their investment portfolios. Understanding these motivations helps explain the growing interest and the strategic approaches these institutions are taking.

One of the primary motivations for investing in cryptocurrencies, particularly Bitcoin, is to hedge against inflation. With central banks around the world adopting expansionary monetary policies, concerns about currency devaluation and inflation have risen. Bitcoin, often referred to as "digital gold," is viewed as a store of value that can protect against the erosion of purchasing power.

Case Study: MassMutual: In December 2020, Massachusetts Mutual Life Insurance Company (MassMutual) made headlines by purchasing $100 million worth of Bitcoin. This move was part of a broader strategy to diversify its investment portfolio and hedge against potential inflation.

MassMutual's investment signaled growing institutional confidence in Bitcoin as a hedge against macroeconomic risks. Their position was that cryptocurrencies offer the potential for significant returns, especially during bull markets. While the high volatility of digital assets can be a concern, it also presents opportunities for substantial gains, which can be particularly attractive in a low-yield environment.

Case Study: Fairfax County Pension Funds: In 2019, two pension funds from Fairfax County, Virginia, invested in blockchain technology and cryptocurrency ventures. The investments, managed through Morgan Creek Capital Management, aimed to capitalize on the high-growth potential of the emerging blockchain and cryptocurrency sectors. These investments highlighted a strategic approach to achieving higher returns while managing risks.

Pension funds and family offices are also motivated by the potential of blockchain technology to revolutionize various industries. By investing in cryptocurrencies and blockchain projects, these institutions can gain exposure to cutting-edge technological innovations that have the potential to transform finance, supply chain management, healthcare, and more.

Case Study: Yale University's endowment, one of the largest in the world, invested in Paradigm, a cryptocurrency-focused venture fund. This investment reflected Yale's recognition of the transformative potential of blockchain technology and its desire to be at the forefront of technological innovation.

They recognized that diversification is a fundamental principle of investment strategy, and cryptocurrencies provide a new avenue for diversification. By including digital assets in their portfolios, pension funds and family offices can spread their investments across a broader range of assets, thereby reducing overall portfolio risk.

Case Study: Norway's Government Pension Fund known as the world's largest sovereign wealth fund, has indirectly invested in Bitcoin through its holdings in MicroStrategy, a company that holds significant Bitcoin reserves. This indirect exposure allows the fund to benefit from the potential upside of cryptocurrencies while maintaining a diversified investment approach.

Strategies for Cryptocurrency Investments

Pension funds and family offices employ various strategies to invest in cryptocurrencies, balancing the need for potential returns with risk management. These strategies include direct investments, indirect exposure, and venture capital investments.

Some pension funds and family offices choose to invest directly in cryptocurrencies like Bitcoin and Ethereum. Direct investments provide the most straightforward exposure to the digital asset market but also come with the highest level of risk and complexity.

Direct investments require secure storage solutions. Institutions often partner with reputable custodial service providers to ensure the safety of their digital assets. These custodians offer features like multi-signature wallets and cold storage to protect against theft and loss.

Ensuring compliance with regulatory requirements is crucial. Institutions need to implement robust KYC and AML procedures and stay abreast of evolving regulations in different jurisdictions.

To mitigate risks associated with direct investments, some institutions seek indirect exposure to cryptocurrencies through investment vehicles like exchange-traded funds

(ETFs), trusts, and publicly traded companies with significant cryptocurrency holdings.

Grayscale Bitcoin Trust (GBTC): The Grayscale Bitcoin Trust is one of the most popular vehicles for gaining indirect exposure to Bitcoin. It allows investors to gain exposure to Bitcoin without having to manage the complexities of holding the asset directly.

Crypto ETFs: In recent years, several cryptocurrency ETFs have been launched, providing a regulated and diversified way for institutions to invest in digital assets. These ETFs offer exposure to a basket of cryptocurrencies, reducing the risk associated with investing in a single asset.

Public Companies: Investing in publicly traded companies with significant cryptocurrency holdings or blockchain initiatives is another way to gain indirect exposure. Companies like MicroStrategy, Tesla, and Square have made substantial investments in Bitcoin, offering investors a way to benefit from the cryptocurrency market through traditional equity investments.

Venture Capital and Private Equity

Another strategy involves investing in venture capital (VC) and private equity funds focused on blockchain technology and cryptocurrency projects. This approach allows institutions to support the growth of innovative startups and gain exposure to the potential upside of early-stage investments.

Andreessen Horowitz, a prominent venture capital firm, has established dedicated funds for investing in blockchain and cryptocurrency projects. By partnering with experienced VC firms, institutions can access a curated portfolio of high-potential startups in the crypto space.

Another example is Sequoia Capital, which has invested in several blockchain and cryptocurrency companies. These investments provide institutions with exposure to cutting-edge developments in the industry and the potential for significant returns.

The involvement of pension funds and family offices has had a profound impact on the cryptocurrency market. Their investments bring significant capital and credibility, contributing to market stability and growth. This is due to the influx of capital from institutional investors which has increased market liquidity, making it easier to execute large trades without causing significant price fluctuations. Higher liquidity contributes to a more stable market environment, attracting even more institutional participants.

The development of institutional-grade trading platforms has facilitated this increased liquidity. Platforms like Coinbase Pro, Gemini, and Kraken offer high liquidity and advanced trading features tailored to the needs of institutional investors.

The participation of reputable institutions like pension funds and family offices has enhanced the credibility of the cryptocurrency market. Their involvement signals to other investors that cryptocurrencies are a legitimate asset class worthy of consideration.

As more institutions enter the market, cryptocurrencies are increasingly seen as mainstream investments. This growing acceptance helps to reduce the stigma and skepticism that have historically surrounded digital assets.

Institutional investors play a crucial role in shaping regulatory developments in the cryptocurrency market. Their need for clear and consistent regulations drives policymakers to establish frameworks that support the growth and stability of the market.

Institutions often engage in advocacy and lobbying efforts

to influence regulatory policies. By working with industry associations and regulatory bodies, they help to shape a more favorable regulatory environment for digital assets.

The capital and support provided by institutional investors catalyze technological innovation in the cryptocurrency space. By investing in blockchain startups and projects, institutions drive the development of new technologies and applications.

Institutional investments fund research and development efforts, leading to advancements in blockchain technology, scalability solutions, and new use cases for cryptocurrencies.

While the future looks promising for cryptocurrency investments by pension funds and family offices, several challenges and uncertainties remain. Despite progress, regulatory uncertainty continues to pose a significant challenge. Governments and regulatory bodies around the world are still grappling with how to effectively regulate cryptocurrencies without stifling innovation.

Achieving global coordination on cryptocurrency regulations has remained a complex task. Different jurisdictions have varying approaches, leading to a fragmented regulatory landscape. The inherent volatility of the cryptocurrency market is another challenge. While volatility can present opportunities for significant gains, it also increases the risk of substantial losses.

Institutions must implement robust risk management strategies to navigate market volatility. This includes diversifying investments, using hedging techniques, and setting appropriate risk limits.

The rapid pace of technological innovation in the cryptocurrency space introduces additional risks. Institutions must stay abreast of technological developments and ensure that their investments are aligned with the most secure and reliable technologies. Cybersecurity threats, including hacking, phishing attacks, and malware, pose significant risks to cryptocurrency investments. Institutions must employ robust cybersecurity measures to protect their assets and sensitive information. The scalability of blockchain networks and the adequacy of infrastructure are critical factors. Institutions need assurance that the underlying technology can support their investment activities without encountering bottlenecks or performance issues.

While significant progress has been made, the cryptocurrency market is still relatively young and evolving. Achieving full maturity will require further development of infrastructure, regulations, and market practices.

Continued institutional adoption will drive further market maturation. As more pension funds and family offices enter the market, the ecosystem will become more sophisticated and resilient.

Education and awareness initiatives are essential for fostering mainstream adoption of cryptocurrencies. Institutions need to understand the risks and opportunities associated with digital assets and blockchain technology fully.

Several pension funds and family offices have been at the forefront of cryptocurrency investments, paving the way for others to follow. These case studies illustrate the diverse approaches and strategies adopted by institutional investors.

Harvard University's Endowment

Harvard University's endowment, one of the largest in the world, has been exploring cryptocurrency investments through indirect exposure. While the university has not disclosed specific details, it is rumored to have invested in cryptocurrency-focused venture capital funds. This approach allows Harvard to gain exposure to the potential upside of blockchain technology while leveraging the expertise of experienced fund managers.

Soros Fund Management

Soros Fund Management, founded by billionaire investor George Soros, has also shown interest in cryptocurrency investments. While Soros himself has expressed skepticism about Bitcoin in the past, the fund reportedly began trading digital assets in 2018. Soros Fund Management's involvement adds credibility to the cryptocurrency market and signals growing institutional acceptance.

Rockefeller Capital Management

Rockefeller Capital Management, a wealth management firm with a storied history, has taken a proactive approach to cryptocurrency investments. The firm offers cryptocurrency exposure to its clients through a partnership with a leading cryptocurrency custody provider. This partnership allows Rockefeller's clients to invest in digital assets while benefiting from the firm's expertise and guidance.

The increasing involvement of pension funds and family offices in the cryptocurrency market represents a significant shift in the financial landscape. These institutions bring substantial capital, credibility, and expertise to the market, driving growth and fostering mainstream acceptance.

While challenges and uncertainties remain, the future looks promising for cryptocurrency investments by institutional investors. Continued regulatory clarity, technological innovation, and market maturation will contribute to the further expansion of institutional involvement.

As pension funds and family offices continue to explore cryptocurrency investments, they will play a crucial role in shaping the future of finance. By embracing digital assets and blockchain technology, these institutions are not only seeking to achieve financial returns but also contributing to the evolution of a more inclusive, efficient, and decentralized financial system.

Chapter 2: The Genesis

The Birth of Bitcoin and Blockchain Technology

The inception of cryptocurrency is marked by the creation of Bitcoin, the first decentralized digital currency, introduced in a whitepaper titled "Bitcoin: A Peer-to-Peer Electronic Cash System" by an anonymous entity known as Satoshi Nakamoto in 2008. The whitepaper outlined a revolutionary new financial system that did not rely on traditional intermediaries such as banks and financial institutions. Instead, Bitcoin transactions would be verified by network nodes through cryptography and recorded on a public ledger known as a blockchain.

Bitcoin was launched in January 2009 with the mining of the genesis block, also known as Block 0, which contained a reward of 50 bitcoins. This marked the beginning of a new era in digital finance. The blockchain technology that underpins Bitcoin ensures transparency and immutability, making it highly secure and resistant to tampering. Every transaction is recorded on a distributed ledger, which is maintained by a decentralized network of computers (nodes) rather than a single central authority.

The early days of Bitcoin were characterized by a lack of understanding and significant skepticism. Many viewed it as a speculative bubble or a fad with no intrinsic value. Initial adoption was primarily driven by enthusiasts and cryptography experts who were fascinated by the potential of a decentralized digital currency. The first notable transaction involving

Bitcoin was the purchase of two pizzas for 10,000 BTC in May 2010, an event now celebrated annually as Bitcoin Pizza Day. At that time, Bitcoin's value was negligible, and it was mostly used for small transactions among early adopters.

The volatility of Bitcoin's price and its association with illegal activities on the dark web, such as the Silk Road marketplace, further fueled skepticism. Traditional financial institutions and regulators were wary of Bitcoin, often viewing it as a threat to the established financial system and a tool for money laundering and other illicit activities.

Despite these challenges, Bitcoin and the broader cryptocurrency ecosystem continued to evolve. Several key milestones helped to shape the perception and adoption of cryptocurrencies over the years:

1. **2011-2013: Emergence of Altcoins:** The success of Bitcoin inspired the creation of alternative cryptocurrencies (altcoins) such as Litecoin, Ripple, and Ethereum. These altcoins introduced new

features and use cases, expanding the potential of blockchain technology beyond digital currency.

2. **2013: Bitcoin Price Surge:** Bitcoin's price surged to over $1,000 for the first time in late 2013, drawing significant media attention and interest from investors. This price surge was partly driven by increased adoption and recognition of Bitcoin's potential as a store of value.

3. **2015: Ethereum and Smart Contracts:** The launch of Ethereum in 2015 introduced the concept of

smart contracts, programmable contracts that automatically execute when certain conditions are met. Ethereum's blockchain enabled decentralized applications (DApps), significantly broadening the scope of blockchain technology.

4. **2017: ICO Boom:** The Initial Coin Offering (ICO) boom in 2017 saw numerous blockchain projects raising funds by issuing new cryptocurrencies. While many projects were legitimate and innovative, the lack of regulation led to widespread

fraud and failures, contributing to a bubble that eventually burst.

5. **2017: Bitcoin Reaches $20,000:** Bitcoin's price reached an all-time high of nearly $20,000 in December 2017, driven by a combination of retail and institutional interest. This milestone further cemented Bitcoin's status as a significant financial asset.

The initial perceptions of Bitcoin and other cryptocurrencies were largely shaped by their volatility and the media's focus on their use in illicit activities. Critics argued that cryptocurrencies lacked intrinsic value, were highly speculative, and posed significant risks to investors. High-profile incidents such as the Mt. Gox exchange hack in 2014, which resulted in the loss of approximately 850,000 bitcoins, reinforced negative perceptions and highlighted the vulnerabilities of the nascent cryptocurrency ecosystem.

Regulators around the world grappled with how to approach cryptocurrencies. Some countries, like China and India, took a hard stance by imposing strict regulations or outright bans on cryptocurrency trading and ICOs. Others, like Japan and Switzerland, adopted more progressive approaches, recognizing the potential benefits of blockchain technology, and working to create regulatory frameworks that would foster innovation while protecting investors.

Despite the widespread skepticism, several innovators and visionaries played crucial roles in advocating for and advancing the development of cryptocurrencies. Figures such as Vitalik Buterin, the cofounder of Ethereum, and Charlie Lee, the creator of Litecoin, were instrumental in pushing the boundaries of what blockchain technology could achieve. Their efforts, along with those of countless developers and entrepreneurs, helped to build a more robust and diverse cryptocurrency ecosystem.

These early innovators were often driven by a belief in the transformative potential of blockchain technology to create a more transparent, efficient, and inclusive financial system. They envisioned a world where individuals could have greater control over their financial assets, conduct transactions without intermediaries, and participate in a global, decentralized economy.

The Rise of Blockchain as a Disruptive Technology

As the cryptocurrency market matured, the underlying blockchain technology began to gain recognition as a disruptive innovation with applications beyond digital currencies. Industries such as supply chain management, healthcare, finance, and real estate started exploring blockchain for its potential to enhance transparency, security, and efficiency.

Blockchain's decentralized nature allows for secure and transparent recording of transactions, which can be particularly beneficial in industries that rely on complex and opaque processes. For example, in supply chain management, blockchain can provide real-time visibility into the movement of goods, reduce fraud, and improve efficiency. In healthcare, blockchain can be used to securely store and share patient records, ensuring data integrity and privacy.

The increasing recognition of blockchain's potential eventually led to growing interest from institutional investors and large financial institutions. Hedge funds, venture capital firms, and even some banks began to explore opportunities in the cryptocurrency space. This institutional interest was a critical factor in legitimizing cryptocurrencies and paving the way for their mainstream adoption.

One of the keys in this journey was the launch of Bitcoin futures by the Chicago Mercantile Exchange (CME) and the Chicago Board Options Exchange (CBOE) in December 2017. These futures contracts provided institutional investors with a regulated and familiar way to gain exposure to Bitcoin, helping to reduce some of the perceived risks associated with direct investment in cryptocurrencies.

Another significant development in the cryptocurrency space has been the rise of decentralized finance (DeFi). DeFi refers to a broad range of financial services, including lending, borrowing, trading, and investing, that are built on blockchain technology and operate without traditional intermediaries. DeFi platforms use smart contracts to automate and execute transactions, providing users with greater control over their assets and reducing reliance on centralized financial institutions.

The DeFi movement has gained substantial traction since 2019, with the total value locked in DeFi protocols reaching billions of dollars. This growth has been driven by the promise of higher yields, greater accessibility, and increased transparency compared to traditional financial services. DeFi has the potential to democratize finance by providing individuals around the world with access to a wide range of financial products and services without the need for a bank account or credit history.

The media has played a significant role in shaping public perception of cryptocurrencies. Initial coverage often focused on the negative aspects, such as volatility, regulatory crackdowns, and security breaches. However, as the market matured and technology evolved, media coverage became more balanced, highlighting both the potential benefits and the risks associated with cryptocurrencies.

High-profile endorsements from influential figures and companies also contributed to shifting public perception. For example, the announcement by Tesla in early 2021 that it had purchased $1.5 billion worth of Bitcoin and would accept it as payment for its vehicles brought significant mainstream attention to cryptocurrencies. Similarly, public statements from figures such as Elon Musk, Jack Dorsey, and institutional investors like Paul Tudor Jones helped to legitimize cryptocurrencies and attract a broader audience.

The Impact of COVID-19 on Cryptocurrency Adoption

The COVID-19 pandemic, which began in early 2020, had a profound impact on

DeFi vs TradFi

global financial markets and accelerated the adoption of digital technologies, including cryptocurrencies. As central banks around the world implemented unprecedented monetary stimulus measures to combat the economic fallout from the pandemic, concerns about inflation and currency devaluation grew. In this context, Bitcoin and other cryptocurrencies were increasingly viewed as a hedge against inflation and a store of value akin to digital gold.

The pandemic also highlighted the vulnerabilities and inefficiencies of traditional financial systems, further driving interest in decentralized financial solutions. The increased reliance on digital payments and remote transactions during lockdowns underscored the need for secure, efficient, and accessible financial services, which cryptocurrencies and blockchain technology could provide.

The cryptocurrency landscape continues to evolve rapidly, driven by technological advancements, regulatory developments, and changing market dynamics. New cryptocurrencies and blockchain projects are constantly emerging, each seeking to address specific use cases and challenges. Innovations such as non-fungible tokens (NFTs), which gained significant popularity in 2021, are expanding the boundaries of what is possible with blockchain technology.

As the market matures, the integration of cryptocurrencies into traditional financial systems is likely to continue. Large financial institutions are increasingly offering cryptocurrency-related products and services, such as custody solutions, trading platforms, and investment funds. This integration is helping to bridge the gap between the traditional financial world and the emerging digital asset ecosystem.

The journey of cryptocurrencies from their inception to their status as a significant financial asset has been marked by innovation, skepticism, and gradual acceptance. The early days of Bitcoin and blockchain technology laid the foundation for a transformative financial revolution that is still unfolding. As the cryptocurrency ecosystem continues to grow and mature, digital assets are reshaping the landscape of global finance. The road to mainstream acceptance has been paved with technological advancements, evolving regulatory frameworks, and increasing institutional interest, all of which have contributed to the gradual integration of cryptocurrencies into traditional investment strategies.

The early pioneers of the cryptocurrency movement played a critical role in driving adoption and innovation. Satoshi Nakamoto's introduction of Bitcoin set the stage for a new era of digital currency, but it was the subsequent contributions of visionaries such as Charles Hoskinson of Cardano and Gavin Wood of Polkadot, have further pushed the boundaries of blockchain technology, focusing on scalability, interoperability, and governance.

Institutional Investment and Market Maturation is one of the most significant developments in the cryptocurrency space and has been the entry of institutional investors. Initially hesitant, institutions have gradually embraced cryptocurrencies as a viable asset class. Factors contributing to this shift include the maturation of the market, the development of robust infrastructure, and the growing recognition of cryptocurrencies as a hedge against inflation and a store of value.

Institutional interest has been evidenced by large-scale investments from hedge funds, asset management firms, and publicly traded companies. For instance, Grayscale Investments has become one of the largest cryptocurrency asset managers, offering a range of investment products that provide exposure to digital assets. Similarly, MicroStrategy, a business intelligence firm, made headlines with its substantial Bitcoin acquisitions, viewing it as a strategic reserve asset.

The launch of Bitcoin futures by established exchanges such as the Chicago Mercantile Exchange (CME) and the Chicago Board Options

Exchange (CBOE) provided institutional investors with a regulated and familiar avenue to gain exposure to Bitcoin. This development was crucial in legitimizing Bitcoin as a financial asset and reducing perceived risks associated with direct cryptocurrency investments.

The regulatory landscape for cryptocurrencies has been dynamic and complex. Initially, many regulators around the world were skeptical or outright hostile towards cryptocurrencies due to concerns about fraud, money laundering, and investor protection. Over time, however, regulatory approaches have evolved, with some jurisdictions adopting more balanced and progressive stances.

In the United States, the Securities and Exchange Commission (SEC) and the Commodity Futures Trading Commission (CFTC) have taken active roles in regulating the cryptocurrency market. The SEC, for instance, has focused on regulating ICOs and ensuring that securities laws are applied to token offerings. Meanwhile, the CFTC has overseen the trading of cryptocurrency derivatives.

Countries like Japan have been pioneers in creating a regulatory framework that supports the growth of the cryptocurrency industry. Japan's Financial Services Agency (FSA) has implemented a comprehensive regulatory regime that includes licensing requirements for cryptocurrency exchanges, anti-money laundering (AML) measures, and consumer protection guidelines. Switzerland, known for its favorable regulatory environment, has attracted numerous blockchain projects and established itself as a global hub for cryptocurrency innovation.

However, regulatory challenges remain, particularly as governments and regulators seek to balance innovation with investor protection and financial stability. The development of clear and consistent regulatory frameworks is essential to foster the continued growth and mainstream adoption of cryptocurrencies.

Technological advancements have been instrumental in addressing some of the early challenges and criticisms of cryptocurrencies, particularly in the areas of security and scalability. The introduction of multi-signature wallets, hardware wallets, and advanced cryptographic techniques has significantly enhanced the security of digital assets. These innovations have made it safer for individuals and institutions to store and transact with cryptocurrencies.

Scalability has also been a critical issue, particularly for

Bitcoin and Ethereum, which have faced limitations in transaction throughput and high fees during periods of high demand. Various solutions have been proposed and implemented to address these challenges. For Bitcoin, the Lightning Network, a second-layer solution, enables faster and cheaper transactions by conducting them off-chain and only settling on the main blockchain when necessary. Ethereum has undergone significant upgrades to improve scalability and performance. The Ethereum 2.0 upgrade, which involves transitioning from a proof-of-work (PoW) to a proof-of-stake (PoS) consensus mechanism, aims to increase transaction throughput, reduce energy consumption, and enhance the overall security of the network. Additionally, layer-2 scaling solutions such as rollups and sidechains are being developed to further enhance Ethereum's capacity.

The Institutionalization of Cryptocurrencies

The increasing institutionalization of cryptocurrencies has brought about significant changes in how digital assets are perceived and managed. Traditional financial institutions, including banks, asset managers, and custodians, have started offering cryptocurrency-related services to meet the growing demand from clients. This trend is driven by a recognition of the potential for cryptocurrencies to diversify portfolios and provide exposure to a new asset class.

Custodial solutions have been a key area of focus, as institutional investors require secure and compliant ways to store large amounts of digital assets. Companies like Fidelity Digital Assets, Coinbase Custody, and BitGo have developed institutional-grade custodial services that provide secure storage, insurance, and regulatory compliance.

Moreover, the development of exchange-traded products (ETPs) and exchange-traded funds (ETFs) that track the performance of cryptocurrencies has made it easier for institutional and retail investors to gain exposure to digital assets. The approval of Bitcoin ETFs in jurisdictions like Canada and Europe has paved the way for similar products in other markets.

In regard to growth, the cryptocurrency market has been accompanied by significant changes in adoption rates and market dynamics. According to various studies and surveys, the number of individuals and institutions holding cryptocurrencies has increased substantially over the past decade. This trend is driven by a combination of factors, including the increasing acceptance of cryptocurrencies as a legitimate asset class, the development of user-friendly platforms, and the growing recognition of blockchain technology's potential. These adoption rates vary significantly by region, with North America, Europe, and Asia leading the way. Countries with advanced financial markets and supportive regulatory environments have seen higher levels of adoption. Additionally, emerging markets have shown significant interest in cryptocurrencies due to their potential to provide financial services to the unbanked and underbanked populations.

The Future of Cryptocurrencies in Institutional Investments

Looking ahead, the future of cryptocurrencies in institutional investments appears promising. As the market continues to mature, and regulatory frameworks become more established, the integration of digital assets into traditional investment portfolios is likely to accelerate. Institutional investors are expected to play a pivotal role in driving the next phase of growth in the cryptocurrency market.

The ongoing development of decentralized finance (DeFi) and other blockchain-based financial services will further expand the use cases and applications of cryptocurrencies. DeFi platforms, which offer a range of financial services without intermediaries, have the potential to disrupt traditional banking and finance. The increasing interest in DeFi from institutional investors highlights the transformative potential of blockchain technology.

For institutions considering or currently investing in cryptocurrencies, several strategic recommendations can help navigate the complex and rapidly evolving landscape:

1. **Diversification:** Diversify investments across different cryptocurrencies and blockchain projects to mitigate risks associated with individual assets.

2. **Due Diligence:** Conduct thorough due diligence on potential investments, including evaluating the technology, team, market

potential, and regulatory environment.

3. **Risk Management:** Implement robust risk management strategies to address the unique risks associated with digital assets, including volatility, cybersecurity, and regulatory changes.

4. **Regulatory Compliance:** Stay informed about regulatory developments and ensure compliance with relevant laws and regulations to avoid legal and reputational risks.

5. Collaboration and Partnerships: Collaborate with established players in the cryptocurrency space, including exchanges, custodians, and technology providers, to leverage their expertise and infrastructure.

6. Education and Training: Invest in education and training for investment teams to build a deep understanding of blockchain technology and digital assets.

The journey of cryptocurrencies from their inception to their status as a significant financial asset class has been marked by innovation, challenges, and gradual acceptance. The early days of Bitcoin and blockchain technology laid the foundation for a transformative financial revolution that is still unfolding. As the cryptocurrency ecosystem continues to grow and mature, digital assets are reshaping the landscape of global finance.

Institutional investors, including pension funds and family offices, are increasingly recognizing the potential of cryptocurrencies to diversify portfolios and provide exposure to a new asset class. With the ongoing development of regulatory frameworks, technological advancements, and market infrastructure, the integration of digital assets into traditional investment strategies is likely to accelerate, paving the way for a more decentralized and inclusive financial future.

Chapter 3: The Early Adopters

The early adopters of cryptocurrency in the world of pension funds and family offices were pioneers who ventured into uncharted territory. They saw potential where others saw risk and laid the groundwork for broader acceptance of digital assets. This chapter explores who these early adopters were, what motivated them to take the plunge, their successes and failures, and the lessons they learned along the way.

Case Study 1: Fairfax County Retirement Systems

One of the first major pension funds to invest in cryptocurrencies was the Fairfax County Retirement Systems in Virginia, USA. This pension fund, which serves county employees, police officers, and firefighters, began investing in blockchain technology and cryptocurrencies in 2019. Their decision was driven by the desire to diversify their investment portfolio and take advantage of the potential high returns associated with digital assets.

The pension fund allocated a small percentage of its assets to cryptocurrency investments, ensuring that the risk to the overall fund was minimized. They invested in blockchain-focused venture capital funds and hedge funds that specialized in cryptocurrencies. This approach allowed them to benefit from the growth of the cryptocurrency market without direct exposure to the volatility of individual cryptocurrencies.

Case Study 2: Family Office of Tim Draper

Tim Draper, a well-known venture capitalist, was one of the earliest high-profile investors in Bitcoin. His family office, Draper Associates, has been investing in cryptocurrencies since 2014. Draper gained significant attention when he purchased nearly 30,000 bitcoins in a government auction of assets seized from the Silk Road marketplace.

Draper's family office continued to invest in various cryptocurrency projects and startups, supporting the growth of the blockchain ecosystem. Draper's early investment in Bitcoin paid off handsomely as the value of Bitcoin surged over the years. His success inspired other family offices to consider cryptocurrency investments as part of their portfolio diversification strategies.

The motivations behind early adoption of cryptocurrencies by pension funds and family offices varied, but several key factors drove their decisions:

1. **Diversification:** Traditional investment

portfolios typically include a mix of stocks, bonds, real estate, and other assets. Early adopters saw cryptocurrencies as a new asset class that could provide diversification benefits. By investing in digital assets, they aimed to reduce their overall risk and enhance potential returns.

2. **Potential for High Returns:** Cryptocurrencies, particularly Bitcoin, have shown the potential for significant price appreciation over time. Early adopters were attracted to the high-risk, high-reward nature of

cryptocurrencies, hoping to achieve substantial gains.

3. **Hedge Against Inflation:** Some early adopters viewed cryptocurrencies as a hedge against inflation and currency devaluation. With central banks around the world implementing expansive monetary policies, concerns about the long-term value of traditional currencies grew. Cryptocurrencies, particularly Bitcoin, were seen as a store of value like gold.

4. **Technological Innovation:** Many early adopters were excited by the

technological innovation represented by blockchain technology. They believed that blockchain could revolutionize various industries, from finance to supply chain management, and wanted to be part of this transformation.

The successes of early adopters varied depending on their investment strategies and the timing of their investments. Here are some key examples of successful outcomes:

1. **Significant Returns:** Early investors in Bitcoin and other

cryptocurrencies saw substantial returns as the prices of these assets increased dramatically over the years. For example, Bitcoin, which was worth less than a dollar in its early days, reached a peak of nearly $20,000 in 2017 and over $60,000 in 2021. Those who invested early reaped enormous profits.

2. **Portfolio Diversification:** By adding cryptocurrencies to their investment portfolios, early adopters achieved greater diversification. This helped to spread risk and potentially enhanced overall

portfolio performance, especially during periods when traditional assets were underperforming.

3. **Increased Innovation:** Investing in blockchain technology and cryptocurrencies also supported the growth and innovation within the industry. Early adopters contributed to the development of new blockchain projects, decentralized applications (DApps), and other technological advancements that have since gained wider acceptance.

Failures and Challenges Faced by Early Adopters

Not all early adopters experienced success; many faced significant challenges and failures. Some of the key issues included:

1. **Volatility:** Cryptocurrencies are notoriously volatile. The price of Bitcoin, for example, has experienced wild swings, often in a short period. Early adopters had to navigate these price fluctuations, which could lead to substantial losses if investments were not carefully managed.

2. **Regulatory Uncertainty:** The regulatory environment for cryptocurrencies has been uncertain and rapidly changing. Early adopters faced the risk of new regulations that could impact their investments negatively. Some countries implemented strict regulations or outright bans, creating additional hurdles.

3. **Security Risks:** The early days of cryptocurrency were plagued by security issues. Hacks, scams, and fraud were common, and many investors lost their assets due to insufficient security measures.

The collapse of the Mt. Gox exchange in 2014, where around 850,000 bitcoins were lost, is one of the most notable examples.

4. **Lack of Understanding:** Many early adopters had limited understanding of the technical aspects and risks associated with cryptocurrencies. This lack of knowledge sometimes led to poor investment decisions and significant losses.

Lessons Learned from Early Adoption

The experiences of early adopters offer valuable lessons for other institutions considering cryptocurrency investments:

1. **Start Small:** Allocating a small percentage of the portfolio to cryptocurrencies can help manage risk. Early adopters who started with a small investment minimized their potential losses while gaining exposure to the new asset class.

2. Diversify Investments: Investing in a range of cryptocurrencies and blockchain projects, rather than putting all funds into a single asset, can help spread risk and increase the chances of achieving positive returns.

3. Conduct Thorough Research: Understanding the technology, market dynamics, and regulatory environment is crucial. Early adopters who conducted thorough research and due diligence were better positioned to navigate the complexities of the cryptocurrency market.

4. Stay Informed About Regulations: Keeping abreast of regulatory developments and ensuring compliance with relevant laws can help avoid legal and reputational risks. Early adopters who stayed informed about the regulatory landscape were better able to adapt to changes.

5. Focus on Security: Implementing robust security measures, such as using hardware wallets and multi-signature solutions, is essential to protect digital assets. Learning from the security failures of early adopters can help prevent losses due to hacks and fraud.

The actions of early adopters had a significant impact on the cryptocurrency industry. Their investments and support helped to legitimize digital assets and attract more attention from other investors and institutions. By demonstrating the potential benefits of cryptocurrency investments, early adopters paved the way for broader acceptance and integration of digital assets into traditional financial systems.

Additionally, the lessons learned from the successes and failures of early adopters have informed the development of best practices and guidelines for future investors. The experiences of these pioneers have contributed to the evolution of the cryptocurrency market, making it more mature and resilient.

As more pension funds and family offices observed the successes of early adopters, the interest in cryptocurrency investments grew. The positive outcomes and lessons learned from early adoption served as powerful testimonials that encouraged other institutions to explore digital assets. This ripple effect led to a gradual increase in the number of pension funds and family offices incorporating cryptocurrencies into their portfolios.

The broader acceptance of cryptocurrencies by traditional financial institutions and regulatory bodies further reinforced this trend. As the market matured and infrastructure improved, it became easier and safer for institutions to invest in digital assets. The development of custodial solutions, regulatory frameworks, and investment products tailored to institutional investors facilitated this broader adoption.

The early adopters of cryptocurrency in the world of pension funds and family offices were trailblazers who took calculated risks to explore a new and unproven asset class. Their motivations varied, but a common thread was the desire for diversification, potential high returns, and participation in technological innovation.

While they faced significant challenges and failures, their successes demonstrated the potential benefits of cryptocurrency investments.

The lessons learned from early adopters have informed the strategies of subsequent investors, helping to navigate the complexities of the cryptocurrency market. The ripple effect of their actions has led to broader acceptance and integration of digital assets into traditional investment portfolios. As the market continues to evolve, the experiences of these pioneers will remain a valuable guide for future investors.

Chapter 4: Crypto Landscape

The journey of cryptocurrencies from a niche innovation to a mainstream financial instrument has been significantly influenced by the regulatory landscapes around the world. Understanding these regulatory environments is crucial for anyone involved in the cryptocurrency market. This chapter delves into how different countries and regions have approached the regulation of digital assets, the impact of these regulations on market participants, and the evolving global trends that shape the future of cryptocurrency regulation.

When Bitcoin first emerged, it was met with curiosity, skepticism, and in many cases, hostility. Governments and financial institutions were unsure how to classify or regulate this new digital currency. The early days were marked by a patchwork of regulatory responses, ranging from outright bans to cautious acceptance.

In the United States, the regulatory approach to cryptocurrencies has been complex and multifaceted.

Various federal agencies, each with their own perspective and jurisdiction, have shaped the landscape.

The Securities and Exchange Commission (SEC) has focused on whether certain cryptocurrencies should be classified as securities. This classification depends on the Howey Test, a legal test derived from a 1946 Supreme Court case. The SEC's scrutiny has been particularly intense regarding Initial Coin Offerings (ICOs), many of which the agency determined were unregistered securities offerings.

Meanwhile, the Commodity Futures Trading Commission (CFTC) classified Bitcoin and other cryptocurrencies as commodities. This classification has significant implications, particularly for the trading of cryptocurrency futures and derivatives. The Internal Revenue Service (IRS) treats cryptocurrencies as property for tax purposes, meaning that each transaction is a taxable event, which adds a layer of complexity for users and investors.

Europe's regulatory approach has been somewhat more cohesive, although individual

DeFi vs TradFi

countries have their own regulations. The European Union (EU) has worked towards creating a harmonized regulatory framework. The Fifth Anti-Money Laundering Directive (5AMLD), which came into effect in 2020, requires cryptocurrency exchanges and wallet providers to implement stringent Know Your Customer (KYC) and Anti-Money Laundering (AML) procedures.

Some countries within the EU, like Germany and Switzerland, have been particularly proactive.

Germany has recognized cryptocurrencies as financial instruments and allows licensed institutions to offer cryptocurrency services. Switzerland, with its "Crypto Valley" in Zug, has established itself as a global hub for blockchain technology, offering a supportive regulatory environment that balances innovation with investor protection.

Asia has shown a wide range of regulatory stances, from stringent bans to progressive acceptance.

China, once home to the largest Bitcoin mining operations and exchanges, has taken a hardline stance against cryptocurrencies. The Chinese government banned ICOs in 2017 and has since taken steps to curtail cryptocurrency trading and mining. Despite these measures, China has been actively exploring the potential of blockchain technology and has been at the forefront of developing a Central Bank Digital Currency (CBDC), known as the Digital Yuan.

In contrast, Japan has been one of the most forward-thinking countries regarding cryptocurrency regulation. Following the high-profile hack of the Mt. Gox exchange in 2014, Japan introduced comprehensive regulations to protect consumers and legitimize the industry. The Financial Services Agency (FSA) oversees the registration and operation of cryptocurrency exchanges, ensuring they adhere to strict standards.

Regulatory actions have a profound impact on the cryptocurrency market. Positive regulatory developments can boost market confidence and drive adoption, while restrictive measures can stifle growth and innovation.

In regions with clear and supportive regulatory frameworks, the cryptocurrency market has flourished. For instance, Japan's regulatory clarity has fostered a thriving ecosystem of exchanges, startups, and institutional investors. Similarly, the regulatory support in Switzerland has attracted numerous blockchain projects and established the country as a leading destination for ICOs and STOs (Security Token Offerings).

These positive regulatory environments have several benefits:

Increased Investor Confidence: Clear regulations provide assurance to investors that their funds are protected and that they are participating in a legitimate market.

Institutional Participation: Well-defined regulatory frameworks encourage institutional investors to enter the market, bringing significant capital and expertise.

Innovation and Development: Supportive regulations create an environment where startups and established companies can innovate without fear of sudden legal repercussions.

Conversely, restrictive, or unclear regulations can have detrimental effects. China's crackdown on cryptocurrency exchanges and mining operations led to a significant drop-in market activity within the country. This move forced many companies to relocate to more favorable jurisdictions, disrupting business operations and the broader market.

Negative regulatory environments can lead to:

Market Volatility: Sudden regulatory changes can cause significant price swings and uncertainty.

Flight of Capital and Talent: Companies and investors often move to more favorable jurisdictions, leading to a brain drain and loss of economic activity in restrictive regions.

Innovation Bottlenecks: Overly stringent regulations can stifle innovation, preventing new technologies and business models from emerging.

As the cryptocurrency market matures, global regulatory trends are becoming more apparent. Countries and regions are learning from each other's experiences and gradually moving towards more harmonized and balanced regulatory approaches.

One of the emerging trends is the harmonization of

regulations across borders.
Organizations like the
Financial Action Task Force
(FATF) are working to
establish global standards for
cryptocurrency regulation.
The FATF's guidelines on
AML and KYC requirements
for cryptocurrency businesses
are being adopted by many
countries, helping to create a
more consistent regulatory
environment worldwide.

International collaboration is
also increasing. Regulatory
bodies are sharing
information and best practices
to tackle issues like money
laundering, fraud, and market

manipulation. This collaborative approach helps to build a more secure and stable global cryptocurrency market.

The Rise of Central Bank Digital Currencies (CBDCs)

Another significant trend is the development of Central Bank Digital Currencies (CBDCs). Many countries are exploring or actively developing digital versions of their national currencies. CBDCs aim to combine the benefits of digital currencies with the stability and trust associated with fiat money.

China's Digital Yuan is the most advanced CBDC project, with pilot programs already underway. The European Central Bank is exploring the Digital Euro, while the Federal Reserve in the United States is also researching the potential for a digital dollar. These initiatives highlight the growing recognition of digital currencies' potential and the desire of governments to maintain control over monetary systems.

The focus of cryptocurrency regulation is also evolving. Initially, regulators were primarily concerned with preventing illicit activities and protecting consumers. While these concerns remain important, regulators are increasingly recognizing the need to foster innovation and support the growth of the digital economy.

For example, the European Union's proposed Markets in Crypto-Assets (MiCA) regulation aims to create a comprehensive framework for cryptocurrency markets, balancing investor protection with the need to support innovation. MiCA seeks to provide legal clarity for issuers and service providers, helping to promote a vibrant and competitive market.

To understand the real-world impact of regulatory approaches, let's look at a few case studies of countries that have taken distinct paths in regulating cryptocurrencies.

In the United States, the regulatory landscape for cryptocurrencies is characterized by a fragmented approach, with multiple agencies involved. This can create confusion and challenges for market participants, but it also allows for a diverse range of regulatory perspectives.

The SEC's focus on whether cryptocurrencies are securities has led to numerous enforcement actions against ICOs that failed to comply with securities laws. This has had a chilling effect on the ICO market in the US, but it has also driven the development of more compliant fundraising models, such as STOs.

The CFTC's oversight of cryptocurrency derivatives has facilitated the growth of regulated futures markets. The approval of Bitcoin futures by the CME and CBOE was a significant milestone, providing institutional investors with a regulated way to gain exposure to Bitcoin.

The IRS's classification of cryptocurrencies as property has introduced tax complexities for users, but it has also clarified the tax treatment of digital assets. Tax reporting requirements have encouraged greater

DeFi vs TradFi

transparency and compliance among cryptocurrency users. Overall, the US approach highlights the importance of clear and consistent regulation while also illustrating the challenges of navigating a complex regulatory environment.

Japan's proactive and supportive regulatory approach has positioned the country as a global leader in the cryptocurrency space. Following the Mt. Gox hack, Japan introduced robust regulations to protect consumers and legitimize the industry.

The Financial Services Agency (FSA) requires cryptocurrency exchanges to register and comply with strict security and AML standards. This regulatory clarity has fostered a thriving ecosystem of exchanges and blockchain startups.

Japan's approach has several key benefits:
The FSA's regulations ensure that exchanges implement strong security measures, reducing the risk of hacks and fraud.

Market Growth: Clear regulations have attracted investment and innovation, helping to grow Japan's cryptocurrency market.

Global Leadership: Japan's supportive stance has established the country as a leader in the global cryptocurrency industry, influencing regulatory approaches in other countries.

China: Strict Control and Innovation

China's approach to cryptocurrency regulation is characterized by strict control and a focus on innovation.

The government has implemented stringent measures to curtail cryptocurrency trading and mining, but it is also actively exploring blockchain technology and developing a CBDC.

China's ban on ICOs and cryptocurrency exchanges in 2017 was a significant move that had a major impact on the global market. Many companies relocated to more favorable jurisdictions, and the domestic market contracted. Despite these restrictions, China has been a pioneer in blockchain innovation. The government's support for blockchain technology has led to significant advancements in various sectors, from supply chain management to finance. The development of the Digital Yuan highlights China's commitment to leading the digital currency revolution.

China's approach further demonstrates the complex relationship between regulation and innovation. While strict control can limit market activity, targeted support for technology can drive significant advancements.

The Role of Industry and Advocacy Groups

Industry and advocacy groups play a crucial role in shaping the regulatory landscape for cryptocurrencies. These organizations work to educate policymakers, advocate for balanced regulations, and support the development of best practices within the industry. Their efforts help to bridge the gap between the rapidly evolving world of digital assets and the traditional financial and regulatory systems.

Various industry associations have emerged to represent the interests of cryptocurrency businesses and investors. These groups engage with regulators, provide input on proposed regulations, and work to promote the growth and stability of the cryptocurrency market.

For example, the Blockchain Association in the United States is an industry group that advocates for a pro-innovation policy environment. It works to ensure that policymakers understand the benefits of blockchain technology and digital assets, and it provides a unified voice for the industry on regulatory issues.

Similarly, in Europe, the European Blockchain Partnership (EBP) is a cooperative initiative that brings together member states to promote blockchain technology. The EBP aims to foster collaboration and develop a trusted European blockchain services infrastructure.

Advocacy organizations also play a key role in shaping the regulatory landscape. These groups often focus on specific aspects of cryptocurrency regulation, such as consumer protection, privacy, and financial inclusion.

Coin Center, a leading non-profit advocacy and research organization based in Washington, D.C., is dedicated to addressing the policy issues facing cryptocurrencies. Coin Center provides detailed research and analysis on regulatory topics, educates policymakers, and advocates for sensible regulation that balances innovation with risk mitigation. The Electronic Frontier Foundation (EFF), an organization focused on digital rights, has also been involved in advocating for privacy and freedom in the use of cryptocurrencies. The EFF works to ensure that regulations do not infringe on individuals' rights to use and develop digital technologies.

The Evolving Role of Central Banks:

Central banks around the world are increasingly recognizing the potential impact of cryptocurrencies and blockchain technology on the financial system. This recognition has led to a range of responses, from the development of regulatory frameworks to the exploration of central bank digital currencies (CBDCs).

Central Bank Digital Currencies (CBDCs)

CBDCs represent a significant shift in how central banks approach digital currencies. Unlike decentralized cryptocurrencies, CBDCs are digital versions of national currencies issued and controlled by central banks. They aim to combine the benefits of digital currencies with the stability and trust associated with traditional fiat money.

Several countries are at the forefront of CBDC development:

China: The Digital Yuan, or Digital Currency Electronic Payment (DCEP), is the most advanced CBDC project. China has conducted extensive pilot programs, testing the Digital Yuan in various cities and for different use cases. The Chinese government aims to use the Digital Yuan to enhance financial inclusion, reduce transaction costs, and maintain control over the monetary system.

European Union: The European Central Bank (ECB) is exploring the Digital Euro. The ECB has conducted public consultations and is working on a comprehensive framework for the potential issuance of a Digital Euro. The primary goals are to provide a secure and efficient digital payment option and to ensure that Europe remains competitive in the digital economy.

United States: The Federal Reserve is researching the potential benefits and risks of a digital dollar. While the US has not yet committed to issuing a CBDC, the Federal Reserve is actively studying the implications for monetary policy, financial stability, and privacy. The development of CBDCs could have significant regulatory implications. Central banks will need to establish frameworks for the issuance, distribution, and use of digital currencies. These frameworks must address key issues such as privacy, security, and interoperability with existing financial systems.

The introduction of CBDCs could also impact the regulatory landscape for decentralized cryptocurrencies. Central banks may seek to assert greater control over the digital currency market, potentially leading to stricter regulations for private cryptocurrencies. At the same time, the coexistence of CBDCs and decentralized cryptocurrencies could drive innovation and competition, benefiting consumers and businesses.

The Path Forward: Balancing Innovation and Regulation

As the cryptocurrency market continues to evolve, finding the right balance between innovation and regulation remains a critical challenge. Policymakers must navigate a complex landscape, ensuring that regulations protect consumers and maintain financial stability without stifling technological advancement.

Key Considerations for Policymakers

Policymakers must consider several key factors when developing cryptocurrency regulations:

Consumer Protection: Ensuring that consumers are protected from fraud, hacks, and other risks is a top priority. Regulations should require robust security measures and clear disclosures from cryptocurrency businesses.

Financial Stability: Policymakers must assess the

potential impact of cryptocurrencies on the broader financial system. This includes monitoring systemic risks and ensuring that the financial infrastructure can support the growth of digital assets.

Innovation and Competitiveness: Regulations should support innovation and competition in the cryptocurrency market. This means providing a clear legal framework that encourages investment and development while maintaining safeguards against abuse.

Global Coordination: Given the global nature of cryptocurrencies, international coordination is essential. Policymakers should work with their counterparts in other countries to develop harmonized regulations and share best practices. Advances in technology can also play a crucial role in supporting effective regulation. Regulatory technology, or "RegTech," leverages digital tools to enhance compliance and oversight. For example, blockchain analytics platforms can help regulators monitor cryptocurrency transactions and detect suspicious activity.

Smart contracts, which are self-executing contracts with terms directly written into code, offer another potential tool for regulatory compliance. Smart contracts can automate regulatory requirements, such as KYC and AML checks, reducing the burden on businesses and improving transparency.

The Future of Self-Regulation is another emerging trend in the cryptocurrency market. Industry participants are developing their own standards and best practices to ensure a secure and trustworthy market. Self-regulatory organizations (SROs) can provide a flexible and adaptive approach to regulation, complementing government oversight.

In Japan, for example, the Japan Virtual Currency Exchange Association (JVCEA) is an SRO that sets standards for cryptocurrency exchanges. The JVCEA works closely with the Financial Services Agency (FSA) to ensure that exchanges comply with regulatory requirements and maintain high standards of security and transparency.

The regulatory landscape for cryptocurrencies is dynamic and evolving, shaped by the actions of governments, central banks, industry groups, and advocacy organizations. Early regulatory reactions varied widely, reflecting the uncertainty and complexity of the new asset class. Over time, however, a more nuanced and balanced approach has emerged.

Positive regulatory developments have fostered market growth and innovation, while restrictive measures have highlighted the challenges of navigating an uncertain environment. As the global trends towards harmonization, collaboration, and the development of CBDCs continue, the regulatory landscape will further mature.

Policymakers face the ongoing challenge of balancing innovation with regulation, ensuring that the cryptocurrency market can grow and thrive while protecting consumers and maintaining financial stability. The experiences of early adopters, the efforts of industry and advocacy groups, and the evolving role of technology all contribute to shaping the future of cryptocurrency regulation.

As the journey of cryptocurrencies continues, understanding and navigating the regulatory landscape will remain a crucial aspect for investors, businesses, and policymakers alike. The path forward requires collaboration, adaptability, and a commitment to fostering a secure, inclusive, and innovative financial ecosystem.

Chapter 5: Institutional Investors

As cryptocurrencies evolved from a fringe interest to a mainstream financial instrument, the need for robust infrastructure to support institutional investment became increasingly apparent. This chapter explores the development of key infrastructure components that enable pension funds and family offices to invest in digital assets safely and efficiently. We will delve into the evolution of custodial services, trading platforms, regulatory compliance tools, and market analytics that form the backbone of institutional involvement in the cryptocurrency market.

One of the primary challenges for institutional investors looking to enter the cryptocurrency market has been the safe storage and management of digital assets. Unlike traditional assets, cryptocurrencies are digital and decentralized, making them susceptible to theft, loss, and hacking. Institutional investors require secure and reliable custodial services to safeguard their investments.

In the early days of cryptocurrency, individuals typically stored their digital assets in personal wallets, often on their computers or hardware devices. While this method worked for small-scale investors, it was impractical and risky for large institutions. The lack of professional custodial solutions deterred many institutional investors from entering the market.

Recognizing this gap, several companies began to develop institutional-grade custodial services. These custodians provide secure storage solutions, often using a combination of cold storage (offline storage) and multi-signature wallets to protect against hacks and unauthorized access. Examples of early custodial service providers include Coinbase Custody, BitGo, and Gemini Custody.

Coinbase Custody, launched in 2018, became one of the most prominent custodial services for institutional investors. By offering a secure storage solution that includes insurance coverage, Coinbase Custody addressed many of the concerns institutions had about the safety of their digital assets. BitGo and Gemini Custody also introduced advanced security features and regulatory compliance measures, further enhancing the trustworthiness of their services.

The Evolution of Custodial Services

As the demand for custodial services grew, these providers expanded their offerings to include additional features and integrations. Modern custodial services now offer a range of tools to facilitate institutional investment: To provide additional protection, many custodians offer insurance policies that cover potential losses due to theft or hacking. This coverage provides peace of mind to institutional investors and mitigates the financial risks associated with storing digital assets.

Custodial services are increasingly focused on ensuring compliance with regulatory requirements. This includes implementing robust KYC (Know Your Customer) and AML (Anti-Money Laundering) procedures, as well as obtaining necessary licenses from financial authorities. To streamline the investment process, custodial services often integrate with trading platforms and other financial infrastructure. This allows institutions to manage their assets, execute trades, and monitor their investments seamlessly from a single interface.

Custodians also provide detailed reporting and auditing tools to help institutional investors track their assets and ensure transparency. These tools are essential for meeting regulatory requirements and maintaining accurate financial records. In addition to secure storage, institutional investors require robust and reliable trading platforms to buy, sell, and manage their digital assets. The development of institutional-grade trading platforms has been crucial for enabling large-scale investment in cryptocurrencies.

Early Trading Platforms

The first cryptocurrency exchanges, such as Mt. Gox and Bitstamp, were primarily designed for retail investors. These platforms lacked the features and security measures necessary to support institutional trading. The collapse of Mt. Gox in 2014, due to a massive hack, highlighted the need for more secure and reliable trading infrastructure.

Emergence of Institutional Trading Platforms

Recognizing the growing interest from institutional investors, several companies began to develop trading platforms specifically tailored to their needs. These platforms introduced features such as high liquidity, advanced trading tools, and regulatory compliance to attract institutional clients.

Coinbase Pro: Originally launched as GDAX (Global Digital Asset Exchange), Coinbase Pro offers a robust trading platform with advanced features such as API access, algorithmic trading, and high liquidity. Coinbase Pro's strong focus on security and regulatory compliance has made it a popular choice among institutional investors.

Gemini Exchange: Founded by the Winklevoss twins, Gemini is another exchange that caters to institutional investors. Gemini emphasizes security and regulatory compliance, being one of the first exchanges to obtain a New York State Department of Financial Services (NYDFS) BitLicense. This regulatory approval has made Gemini a trusted platform for institutions.

Kraken: Known for its comprehensive range of cryptocurrencies and advanced trading features, Kraken has also made significant strides in appealing to institutional investors. Kraken offers high liquidity, futures trading, and OTC (over the counter) services, making it a versatile platform for large-scale trading.

Institutional trading platforms differ from retail-focused exchanges in several keyways:

High Liquidity: To facilitate large trades without significantly impacting market prices, institutional platforms provide deep liquidity. This is achieved through partnerships with liquidity providers and market makers.

Advanced Trading Tools: Institutions require sophisticated trading tools such as algorithmic trading, futures, and options. These tools allow for more strategic and efficient trading strategies.

API Access: Application Programming Interfaces (APIs) enable institutions to integrate their trading systems directly with the exchange. This allows for automated trading and real-time data access.

Security and Compliance: Enhanced security measures, including multi-factor authentication and cold storage, are crucial. Regulatory compliance is also a priority, ensuring that the platform meets legal standards for AML and KYC. For institutional investors, regulatory compliance is not just a legal requirement but also a matter of reputation and operational integrity. The complexity and global nature of cryptocurrency markets necessitate sophisticated tools to ensure compliance with various regulations.

Initially, compliance was managed manually, which was time-consuming and prone to errors. As the industry grew, the need for automated and reliable compliance solutions became apparent. This led to the development of RegTech (Regulatory Technology) tools specifically designed for the cryptocurrency market.

Key Components of Compliance Tools

KYC (Know Your Customer): KYC processes are essential for verifying the identities of clients and preventing fraudulent activities. Advanced KYC tools use artificial intelligence and machine learning to verify identities quickly and accurately, reducing the burden on compliance teams.

AML (Anti-Money Laundering): AML tools are designed to detect and prevent money laundering activities. These tools analyze transaction patterns and flag suspicious activities for further investigation. They are essential for meeting regulatory requirements and ensuring the integrity of the financial system.

Transaction Monitoring: Continuous monitoring of transactions helps identify unusual or suspicious activities in real-time. This is critical for detecting potential fraud, money laundering, or other illicit activities.

Regulatory Reporting: Compliance tools often include features for generating regulatory reports. These reports help institutions meet their legal obligations and provide transparency to regulators. Several companies have developed comprehensive compliance solutions for the cryptocurrency market:

Chainalysis: Chainalysis is a leading blockchain analysis company that provides AML and compliance solutions. Its tools allow institutions to track and analyze blockchain transactions, ensuring compliance with regulatory requirements.

Elliptic: Elliptic offers blockchain analytics and transaction monitoring solutions. Its tools help institutions detect and prevent illicit activities, ensuring that their operations remain compliant with global regulations.

CipherTrace: CipherTrace provides cryptocurrency

intelligence and compliance solutions. Its platform helps institutions identify and mitigate risks, ensuring that they meet regulatory standards.

Market Analytics and Data Services

Institutional investors rely on accurate and timely market data to make informed investment decisions. The development of sophisticated market analytics and data services has been crucial in supporting institutional involvement in the cryptocurrency market.

In the early days of cryptocurrency, market data was fragmented and often unreliable. Investors had to rely on multiple sources to piece together a comprehensive view of the market. This lack of reliable data made it difficult for institutions to make informed decisions and assess market risks. As the market matured, several companies began to offer comprehensive market data services tailored to the needs of institutional investors. These services provide real-time data, advanced analytics, and historical market information.

Key Features of Market Data Services

Real-Time Data: Access to real-time market data is crucial for making timely investment decisions. Data services provide real-time price feeds, trading volumes, and order book data from multiple exchanges. Institutions require advanced analytics to identify trends, assess risks, and develop trading strategies. Market data services offer tools such as charting, technical analysis, and sentiment analysis. Additionally, access to historical market data allows institutions to back test trading strategies and analyze long-term trends. This data is essential for developing robust investment models.

Market Research and Insights: In addition to raw data, market data services often provide research reports and insights from industry experts. These reports help institutions stay informed about market developments and emerging trends. Several companies have emerged as leaders in providing market data and analytics for the cryptocurrency market:

CoinMarketCap:
CoinMarketCap is one of the most widely used sources for cryptocurrency market data. It provides real-time price information, market capitalization, and trading volumes for thousands of cryptocurrencies. CryptoCompare offers comprehensive market data, including real-time price feeds, historical data, and advanced analytics. Its platform is used by both retail and institutional investors to track market trends and make informed decisions. Lastly, Kaiko provides institutional-grade market data and

analytics. Its services include real-time and historical data, order book data, and advanced analytics tools.

Integration and Interoperability

For institutional investors, the seamless integration of custodial services, trading platforms, compliance tools, and market data services is essential. This integration ensures that all components of the investment process work together efficiently and securely.

Chapter 6: Minting Our Own

The concept of institutions like pension funds minting their own cryptocurrency, particularly in the form of a coin owned by their members, is a novel and intriguing proposition. As the world of finance continues to be disrupted by blockchain technology and digital assets, this idea warrants a thorough examination. This narrative explores the potential benefits, challenges, and implications of pension funds creating and managing their own cryptocurrency, ultimately providing a comprehensive view of whether this innovative approach is advisable.

Pension funds are large, institutional investors responsible for managing the retirement savings of millions of individuals. Their primary objective is to ensure the financial security of their members by investing in a diverse range of assets, including stocks, bonds, real estate, and increasingly, alternative investments like private equity and hedge funds.

Cryptocurrencies, on the other hand, are digital or virtual currencies that use cryptography for security and operate on decentralized networks based on blockchain technology. Bitcoin, the first and most well-known cryptocurrency, was introduced in 2009, and since then, thousands of cryptocurrencies have emerged, each with unique features and use cases.

The Case for Pension Funds Minting Their Own Cryptocurrency

One of the most compelling arguments for pension funds to mint their own cryptocurrency is the potential to enhance member engagement and foster a sense of ownership. By issuing a coin owned by the members, pension funds can create a direct link between the fund's performance and the members' financial interests. This could lead to increased transparency and accountability, as members would have a vested interest in the fund's investment strategies and outcomes.

Traditional pension fund investments are often illiquid and inaccessible until retirement. By creating a cryptocurrency, pension funds could offer a more liquid and accessible asset to their members. Members could potentially trade these coins on secondary markets, providing them with flexibility and access to their retirement savings if needed.

Minting their own cryptocurrency could provide pension funds with an additional tool for diversification and risk management. By integrating digital assets into their portfolios, pension funds can potentially reduce overall portfolio risk through diversification, given the low correlation between cryptocurrencies and traditional asset classes.

A pension fund-backed cryptocurrency could pave the

way for innovative financial products and services. For example, the cryptocurrency could be used as collateral for loans, enabling members to access credit without liquidating their traditional retirement investments. Additionally, the cryptocurrency could be integrated into decentralized finance (DeFi) platforms, offering members access to yield farming, staking, and other DeFi services.

Regulatory Uncertainty:

The regulatory environment

for cryptocurrencies is still evolving, and the introduction of a pension fund-backed cryptocurrency would undoubtedly attract significant regulatory scrutiny. Pension funds would need to navigate complex regulatory frameworks to ensure compliance with securities laws, tax regulations, and consumer protection standards. Failure to do so could result in legal challenges and financial penalties.

Cryptocurrencies are susceptible to hacking and

cyber-attacks. Pension funds would need to invest heavily in robust security measures to protect their digital assets and ensure the safety of their members' investments. This includes secure custody solutions, multi-signature wallets, and continuous security audits. The reputational risk associated with potential security breaches cannot be underestimated.

Cryptocurrencies are known for their high volatility, which could pose significant risks for pension funds. The value of the pension fund-backed cryptocurrency could fluctuate widely, potentially impacting the stability of the fund and the financial security of its members. Pension funds would need to develop strategies to manage this volatility and ensure that their core mission of providing stable, long-term retirement benefits is not compromised.

The creation and management of a cryptocurrency requires substantial operational expertise and resources.

Pension funds would need to invest in blockchain technology, hire skilled professionals, and develop new operational processes to support the issuance, trading, and management of their cryptocurrency. This could divert resources from their core investment activities and introduce additional operational risks.

Blockchain Selection:

Choosing the right blockchain platform is a critical decision. Pension funds need to consider factors such as security, scalability, transaction costs, and interoperability with other blockchain networks. Established platforms like Ethereum, Binance Smart Chain, or emerging enterprise solutions like Hyperledger and Corda could be viable options, depending on the specific needs and objectives of the pension fund.

Smart contracts are self-executing contracts with the terms of the agreement directly written into code. They are essential for automating various processes related to the issuance, trading, and management of the cryptocurrency. Pension funds would need to collaborate with experienced blockchain developers to design and implement smart contracts that meet their requirements while ensuring security and compliance.

Member Education and Communication:

Introducing a new cryptocurrency requires effective communication and education efforts to ensure that members understand the benefits and risks involved. Pension funds would need to develop comprehensive educational materials, conduct workshops, and provide ongoing support to help members navigate this new investment landscape. Clear and transparent communication is essential to build trust and confidence among members.

Collaborating with established players in the cryptocurrency and blockchain space can provide valuable expertise and resources. Pension funds could partner with cryptocurrency exchanges, DeFi platforms, and blockchain technology providers to leverage their experience and infrastructure. These partnerships can also help in managing regulatory compliance and security challenges.

While the concept of pension funds minting their own cryptocurrency is still largely theoretical, there are some related examples and initiatives that provide valuable insights.

1. Central Bank Digital Currencies (CBDCs):

Several central banks worldwide are exploring or have already launched their own digital currencies. For example, China's Digital Yuan and the European Central Bank's Digital Euro initiatives demonstrate how large, institutional entities can successfully issue and manage digital currencies. These initiatives provide valuable lessons in regulatory compliance, security, and operational management that pension funds can learn from.

2. Corporate Cryptocurrencies:

Some corporations have experimented with issuing their own cryptocurrencies. For instance, Facebook's Diem (formerly Libra) project aimed to create a stablecoin backed by a basket of currencies. While Diem faced significant regulatory hurdles, it highlighted the potential benefits and challenges of creating a corporate-backed cryptocurrency.

3. Tokenized Investment Funds:

Some investment funds have tokenized their assets, allowing investors to buy and trade tokens representing shares in the fund. For example, the Neufund platform has facilitated the tokenization of equity in various companies, providing a glimpse into how traditional assets can be integrated with blockchain technology. Pension funds can draw inspiration from these examples to design and implement their own cryptocurrency.

By minting their own cryptocurrency, pension funds can empower their members by giving them greater control over their retirement savings. Members can actively participate in the governance of the cryptocurrency, vote on key decisions, and benefit from the fund's success. This democratization of financial management aligns with the broader trend of decentralized finance and member-centric investment models.

A pension fund-backed cryptocurrency can enhance financial inclusion by providing members with access to digital financial services that were previously inaccessible. This is particularly relevant for members in developing countries or underserved communities who may lack access to traditional banking services. The cryptocurrency can facilitate low-cost, cross-border transactions, enabling members to manage their retirement savings more effectively.

Pension funds increasingly prioritize environmental, social, and governance (ESG) factors in their investment decisions. The creation of a cryptocurrency should align with these values. Pension funds can ensure that their cryptocurrency operates on energy-efficient blockchain platforms and supports sustainable development goals. Additionally, they can use the cryptocurrency to incentivize sustainable behaviors and investments among their members.

The idea of pension funds minting their own cryptocurrency is undoubtedly ambitious and fraught with challenges. However, it also presents a unique opportunity to innovate and enhance the way retirement savings are managed. By carefully navigating the regulatory, security, and operational hurdles, pension funds can create a cryptocurrency that provides tangible benefits to their members.

Soon, we can expect to see

more experimentation and pilot projects as pension funds explore the feasibility of issuing their own digital assets. Successful implementation will require a collaborative effort involving regulators, blockchain developers, financial institutions, and, most importantly, the members themselves.

Ultimately, the decision to mint a pension fund-backed cryptocurrency should be guided by a clear understanding of the potential benefits and risks, a commitment to transparency and member engagement, and a strategic vision for the future of retirement savings. If done right, this innovative approach could redefine the relationship between pension funds and their members, creating a more dynamic, inclusive, and resilient financial ecosystem.

Chapter 7: The Rising Tide

The cryptocurrency market has witnessed a seismic shift in recent years as institutional investors have increasingly recognized the potential of digital assets. This chapter explores the factors driving institutional interest in cryptocurrencies, the evolving investment landscape, and the implications for the broader financial industry. From hedge funds to asset managers, institutional players are diving deep into the crypto space, reshaping the market, and paving the way for mainstream adoption.

The journey of institutional investors into the crypto space has been marked by skepticism, exploration, and ultimately, adoption. Initially dismissed as a speculative bubble or a niche market, cryptocurrencies have gradually gained acceptance among institutional players seeking diversification, alpha generation, and exposure to transformative technologies.

In the early days of Bitcoin, institutional interest was tepid at best. Skeptical of the nascent asset's legitimacy and volatility, many traditional investors viewed cryptocurrencies as a speculative fad with little long-term value. High-profile hacks, regulatory uncertainty, and the association with illicit activities further deterred institutional participation.

Jamie Dimon, CEO of JPMorgan Chase, famously called Bitcoin a "fraud" in 2017, igniting a debate within the financial community about the legitimacy of cryptocurrencies. Dimon's comments reflected widespread skepticism among traditional bankers and investors. Regulatory ambiguity surrounding cryptocurrencies added another layer of uncertainty for institutional investors. The lack of clear guidelines and oversight left many institutions wary of regulatory backlash or legal risks associated with crypto investments. Despite initial skepticism, some forward-thinking institutions began to explore the potential of cryptocurrencies and blockchain technology.

Venture capital firms, tech companies, and progressive asset managers have started allocating capital to crypto-focused funds and projects, laying the groundwork for broader institutional involvement.

Venture capital firms like Andreessen Horowitz and Union Square Ventures were among the early backers of blockchain startups, recognizing the disruptive potential of decentralized technologies. These investments provided a bridge between the traditional financial world and the emerging crypto ecosystem. Tech giants like IBM and Microsoft forged partnerships with blockchain projects to explore applications beyond cryptocurrencies. These collaborations signaled growing institutional interest in blockchain technology as a catalyst for innovation across industries.

In recent years, institutional interest in cryptocurrencies has reached new heights, driven by a combination of macroeconomic factors, technological advancements, and evolving market dynamics. From hedge funds to pension funds, institutions are increasingly allocating capital to digital assets as part of their investment strategies.

Several key factors have contributed to the growing interest of institutional investors in the crypto space, reshaping the investment landscape and driving market evolution.

Macro-economic trends, including unprecedented monetary stimulus, low interest rates, and inflationary pressures, have fueled institutional interest in alternative assets like cryptocurrencies. With traditional hedges like bonds offering diminishing returns, institutions are seeking alternative stores of value and inflation hedges. Central bank interventions, such as quantitative easing programs, have flooded the market with liquidity, raising concerns about currency devaluation and inflationary risks. Cryptocurrencies, with their limited supply and deflationary properties also offer a potential hedge against fiat currency depreciation.

Persistently low interest rates have driven investors to explore higher-yielding assets, including cryptocurrencies. With yields on traditional fixed-income investments at historic lows, institutions are turning to alternative investments like Bitcoin and Ethereum for potential alpha generation. The maturation of institutional infrastructure, including custody solutions, trading platforms, and regulatory frameworks, has played a pivotal role in attracting institutional capital to the crypto space. Robust custodial services, compliant trading platforms, and regulatory clarity have reduced barriers to entry for institutional investors.

Custodial Solutions: The emergence of reputable custodial solutions, offering secure storage and insurance coverage for digital assets, has addressed one of the key concerns of institutional investors. Institutions can now safely store and manage cryptocurrencies, mitigating the risk of theft or loss. Increasing regulatory clarity, particularly in jurisdictions like the United States and Europe, has provided institutions with a clearer roadmap for compliance and investment. Regulatory frameworks governing cryptocurrencies and blockchain technology have evolved, offering a more stable and predictable environment for institutional participation.

The development of institutional grade trading platforms, offering advanced trading tools, liquidity, and compliance features, has facilitated large-scale investment in cryptocurrencies. These platforms provide institutions with the infrastructure needed to execute trades and manage portfolios efficiently. The maturation of the cryptocurrency market, marked by increased liquidity, reduced volatility, and growing investor confidence, has made digital assets more appealing to institutional investors. As the market matures, institutional players are gaining greater confidence in the reliability and stability of cryptocurrencies as an asset class. This influx of institutional capital has led to increased liquidity in the cryptocurrency market, making it easier for institutions to enter and exit positions without significantly impacting prices. Higher liquidity reduces transaction costs and market frictions, making cryptocurrencies more attractive to institutional investors.

While cryptocurrencies are still known for their volatility, the overall volatility of the market has decreased over time as institutional participation has grown. Institutional investors, with their longer time horizons and risk management strategies, contribute to market stability and dampen volatility.

The development of a robust derivatives market, including futures, options, and other derivative products, has provided institutional investors with additional tools for managing risk and executing sophisticated trading strategies. Derivatives markets offer institutions exposure to cryptocurrencies without the need to hold the underlying assets directly.

Institutional investors employ various investment strategies when entering the crypto space, ranging from long-term buy-and-hold approaches to active trading strategies. These strategies reflect institutions' diverse risk appetites, investment mandates, and market outlooks. Many institutional investors adopt a long-term buy-and-hold approach when investing in cryptocurrencies, treating digital assets as a strategic allocation within their investment portfolios. These institutions view cryptocurrencies as a store of value and a hedge against inflation, holding positions for the medium to long term.

Institutions strategically allocate a portion of their investment portfolios to cryptocurrencies, typically Bitcoin and Ethereum, based on their risk tolerance and investment objectives. These allocations serve as a hedge against systemic risks and a potential source of uncorrelated returns.

Cryptocurrencies offer diversification benefits, with low correlation to traditional asset classes like stocks and bonds. By including digital assets in their portfolios, institutions can reduce overall portfolio risk and enhance risk-adjusted returns.

Active Trading Strategies

Some institutional investors engage in active trading strategies, seeking to capitalize on short-term market inefficiencies, price discrepancies, and volatility. These institutions employ sophisticated trading algorithms, quantitative models, and technical analysis to execute trades and generate alpha. Another strategy is Algorithmic trading, which is powered by advanced algorithms and quantitative models, enable institutions to automate trade execution and capitalize on market inefficiencies. These strategies can be tailored to various market conditions and trading objectives, providing institutions with a competitive edge in the market.

Arbitrage Opportunities within the Cryptocurrency markets are known for their fragmentation and inefficiencies, creating arbitrage opportunities for savvy traders. Institutional investors leverage these opportunities by exploiting price differentials across different exchanges and liquidity pools, profiting from temporary price disparities.

Quantitative trading strategies is another preference and uses statistical analysis and mathematical models to identify trading opportunities and generate alpha. These strategies analyze historical data, market trends and indicators to inform trading decisions, allowing institutions to profit from short-term price movements.

In addition to long-term holdings and active trading strategies, some institutional investors pursue opportunistic investments in the crypto space, capitalizing on specific market trends, events, or developments. These investments may include participation in token sales, venture capital investments, or strategic partnerships with blockchain projects.
Token Sales and ICOs, Initial coin offerings (ICOs) and token sales present

opportunities for institutional investors to gain exposure to innovative blockchain projects at an early stage. Institutions evaluate the potential of these projects based on factors such as technology, team, market demand, and regulatory compliance.

As mentioned in previous chapters, Venture Capital Investments are geared towards the Institutional venture capital firms allocation of capital to blockchain startups and cryptocurrency projects with high growth potential. These investments provide institutions with exposure to cutting-edge technologies and disruptive business models, potentially delivering significant returns over the long term.

Strategic Partnerships
Institutions form strategic partnerships with blockchain projects, contributing capital, expertise, and resources in exchange for access to technology, talent, and market opportunities. These partnerships enable institutions to leverage blockchain innovations and integrate them into their

existing operations or investment strategies.

The growing interest of institutional investors in the crypto space has profound implications for the broader financial industry, reshaping traditional investment paradigms, market dynamics, and regulatory frameworks. Institutional participation contributes to the evolution and maturation of the cryptocurrency market, fostering greater liquidity, efficiency, and stability. As institutions bring their expertise, capital, and institutional-grade infrastructure into the crypto space, the market becomes more resilient and attractive to a broader range of investors.

Market Liquidity partnered with Institutional involvement increases liquidity in the cryptocurrency market, reducing spreads and transaction costs for all participants. Higher liquidity attracts more institutional players, creating a virtuous cycle of market growth and maturity. Institutional trading activity enhances price discovery mechanisms in cryptocurrency markets, making prices more reflective of supply and demand dynamics. Transparent and efficient price discovery facilitates risk management, investment decision-making, and market efficiency.

Regulatory Considerations

The influx of institutional capital into the crypto space has prompted regulators to reevaluate their approach to cryptocurrencies and blockchain technology. Regulators seek to strike a balance between fostering innovation and protecting investors, addressing concerns

related to market integrity, investor protection, and systemic risks.
Regulatory clarity is essential for institutional investors to operate confidently in the crypto space. Clear and consistent regulations provide institutions with a roadmap for compliance, reducing legal risks and uncertainty. Regulators may introduce regulations specifically tailored to institutional investors participating in the crypto space, addressing concerns related to custody, trading, disclosure, and investor protection. These regulations aim to safeguard

institutional assets and maintain market integrity.

Let's not forget the convergence of traditional finance in the crypto space, which accelerates as institutional players embrace digital assets and blockchain technology. Financial institutions, asset managers, and service providers increasingly offer cryptocurrency products and services, bridging the gap between traditional and crypto markets. Financial institutions launch new products and services tailored to institutional investors, including cryptocurrency custody, trading, lending, and asset management solutions. These products enable institutions to access digital assets while complying with regulatory requirements and risk management standards. Traditional financial intermediaries, such as banks, brokerage firms, and asset managers, expand their offerings to include cryptocurrency-related services. These intermediaries facilitate institutional participation in the crypto space, providing expertise, infrastructure, and regulatory compliance support.

Global Adoption and Accessibility

Institutional involvement drives global adoption and accessibility of cryptocurrencies, making digital assets more accessible to investors worldwide. Institutional-grade infrastructure, regulatory compliance, and market liquidity contribute to broader acceptance and adoption of cryptocurrencies as a legitimate asset class. Institutional capital flows into the crypto space from diverse geographic regions, driving global adoption and liquidity.

As institutions allocate capital to digital assets, the market becomes more interconnected, accessible, and resilient to regional fluctuations and geopolitical risks.
Mainstream Acceptance is key for the Institutional endorsement of cryptocurrencies and blockchain technology. This promotes mainstream acceptance and awareness. As institutional investors validate the legitimacy and potential of digital assets, retail investors, businesses, and governments increasingly embrace

cryptocurrencies as part of the global financial ecosystem.

The growing interest of institutional investors in the crypto space marks a transformative shift in the financial landscape, reshaping investment paradigms, market dynamics, and regulatory frameworks. From hedge funds to asset managers, institutions are recognizing the potential of cryptocurrencies as a new asset class offering diversification, alpha generation, and exposure to transformative technologies.

As institutional participation continues to expand, the crypto space will undergo further evolution and maturation, fostering greater liquidity, efficiency, and mainstream acceptance. Regulatory clarity, institutional infrastructure, and market integration will play key roles in shaping the future of cryptocurrencies and blockchain technology as integral components of the global financial system.

Chapter 8: Institutional Interest

As the financial landscape continues to evolve, institutional investors, including pension funds, are increasingly considering the inclusion of cryptocurrency in their portfolios. This shift is driven by a variety of factors, each contributing to the growing acceptance and integration of digital assets into traditional investment strategies. One of the primary reasons pension funds are exploring cryptocurrency investments is diversification. Traditional assets such as stocks, bonds, and real estate have long dominated institutional portfolios. However, the unique characteristics of cryptocurrencies offer an opportunity to diversify beyond these conventional assets. Cryptocurrencies have shown low correlation with traditional asset classes, meaning their price movements are often independent of stocks and bonds. This low correlation can help mitigate overall portfolio risk and enhance returns, especially in volatile market conditions.

For instance, during periods of economic downturn, when traditional markets suffer, cryptocurrencies have sometimes demonstrated resilience or even positive performance. This potential to act as a hedge against market fluctuations is particularly attractive to pension funds, which are tasked with managing long-term financial stability for their beneficiaries.

High Return Potential

Cryptocurrencies have gained attention due to their potential for high returns. Bitcoin, for example, has experienced significant appreciation since its inception, offering early adopters substantial profits. While the high volatility of cryptocurrencies poses a risk, it also presents an opportunity for outsized gains. Pension funds, with their typically conservative investment strategies, are beginning to allocate a small percentage of their assets to cryptocurrencies, viewing it as a high-risk, high-reward component that could boost overall portfolio performance.

The success stories of institutional investors who have already ventured into the cryptocurrency market further fuel interest. Notable examples include companies like MicroStrategy and Tesla, whose investments in Bitcoin have garnered substantial returns. These high-profile cases provide a compelling argument for pension funds to consider a cautious yet strategic entry into crypto space.

Inflation Hedge

In the current economic environment, characterized by unprecedented monetary policy measures and rising inflation concerns, cryptocurrencies are seen as a potential hedge against inflation. Unlike fiat currencies, which can be devalued by central banks' policies, cryptocurrencies like Bitcoin have a capped supply. Bitcoin's fixed supply of 21 million coins introduces a scarcity element, akin to precious metals like gold, which have traditionally been used as inflation hedges.

Institutional investors, including pension funds, are drawn to this characteristic, as it provides a means to protect their portfolios from the eroding effects of inflation. As fiat currencies lose purchasing power, assets with inherent scarcity can maintain or even increase in value, preserving the real value of investments.

Institutional Acceptance and Regulatory Clarity

The growing acceptance of cryptocurrencies by major financial institutions and the increasing clarity in regulatory frameworks are significant factors influencing pension funds' interest. In recent years, prominent financial institutions like Fidelity, Goldman Sachs, and JPMorgan have launched cryptocurrency-related products and services, signaling a broader acceptance within the financial industry. This institutional endorsement lends credibility to cryptocurrencies and reassures conservative investors about their legitimacy and potential.

Moreover, regulatory developments have made the cryptocurrency market more accessible and safer for institutional investors. Governments and regulatory bodies worldwide are working to establish clear guidelines and regulations for cryptocurrency trading, custody, and taxation. For instance, the U.S. Securities and Exchange Commission (SEC) has taken steps to regulate cryptocurrency exchanges and ensure investor protection. Such regulatory clarity reduces the perceived risks associated with cryptocurrencies and encourages pension funds to explore this asset class more confidently.

Technological Advancements and Infrastructure

The maturation of cryptocurrency infrastructure and technological advancements have also played a crucial role in attracting institutional investors. The development of secure and reliable custody solutions, such as those offered by Coinbase Custody and Fidelity Digital Assets, addresses one of the primary concerns of institutional investors: the safe storage of digital assets. These custodial services provide institutional-grade security measures, including multi-signature wallets, cold storage, and insurance coverage, mitigating the risk of theft or loss.

Additionally, the emergence of regulated cryptocurrency exchanges and trading platforms has improved market liquidity and transparency. Platforms like Coinbase, Kraken, and Gemini offer institutional investors access to deep liquidity pools and advanced trading tools, facilitating large transactions without significant market impact. This enhanced infrastructure makes it easier for pension funds to enter and exit positions in the cryptocurrency market, further reducing the barriers to entry.

Strategic Long-Term Perspective

Pension funds are inherently long-term investors, with investment horizons that span decades. This long-term perspective aligns well with the potential growth trajectory of cryptocurrencies. While the market remains volatile, the underlying blockchain technology and the increasing adoption of digital currencies suggest significant long-term growth potential. Institutional investors recognize that the cryptocurrency market is still in its early stages, and by entering now, they can position themselves to benefit from future developments and innovations.

Furthermore, the integration of blockchain technology into various industries, such as finance, supply chain management, and healthcare, is expected to drive widespread adoption and increase the value of associated cryptocurrencies. By investing in cryptocurrencies, pension funds can gain exposure to this transformative technology and its potential to reshape the global economy.

Peer Pressure and Competitive Advantage

As more institutional investors allocate funds to cryptocurrencies, a form of peer pressure emerges within the industry. Pension funds that observe their peers successfully navigating the cryptocurrency market may feel compelled to follow suit to maintain a competitive advantage. Failing to do so could result in missed opportunities and potentially lag industry trends.

The competitive landscape of the investment world

encourages pension funds to explore innovative investment strategies. By incorporating cryptocurrencies into their portfolios, pension funds can differentiate themselves and demonstrate their commitment to staying at the forefront of financial innovation. This proactive approach can attract new investors and beneficiaries who value forward-thinking and progressive investment strategies.

Evolving Risk Perception

The perception of risk associated with cryptocurrencies is evolving. Initially, cryptocurrencies were often associated with illicit activities and extreme volatility. However, as the market matures and regulatory frameworks improve, the perceived risk is diminishing. Institutional investors are becoming more comfortable with the idea of including cryptocurrencies in their portfolios as they gain a better understanding of the asset class and its potential benefits.

Educational initiatives and research reports from reputable financial institutions are also contributing to this shift in perception. Comprehensive analyses and case studies that highlight the performance and risk characteristics of cryptocurrencies provide valuable insights for pension fund managers. Armed with this information, they can make more informed decisions about the potential role of cryptocurrencies in their investment strategies.

The growing interest of pension funds in

cryptocurrencies is driven by a combination of factors that align with their long-term investment objectives and risk management strategies. Diversification, high return potential, and the ability to hedge against inflation make cryptocurrencies an attractive addition to traditional portfolios. The increasing institutional acceptance, regulatory clarity, and advancements in infrastructure further enhance the appeal of digital assets.

Moreover, the strategic long-term perspective of pension funds, combined with the evolving perception of risk and competitive pressures, encourages exploration and adoption of cryptocurrencies. As the financial landscape continues to evolve, pension funds recognize the need to adapt and embrace innovative investment opportunities to secure the financial future of their beneficiaries. By carefully navigating the cryptocurrency market, pension funds can position themselves to benefit from the transformative potential of digital assets and ensure the sustainability and growth of their portfolios.

Chapter 9: Portfolio Expansion

As institutional investors like pension funds contemplate expanding their portfolios to include cryptocurrencies, the process involves meticulous planning, extensive research, and strategic implementation. Given their fiduciary responsibilities and the need to safeguard the financial well-being of their beneficiaries, pension funds approach this transition with caution and due diligence. This narrative outlines the comprehensive steps involved in integrating cryptocurrencies into their investment strategies.

The journey begins with recognizing the potential benefits of incorporating cryptocurrencies into the portfolio. Pension fund managers, often influenced by the evolving financial landscape and emerging investment trends, start by identifying the key motivations behind this move. These motivations typically include the desire for diversification, the potential for high returns, an effective hedge against inflation, and the need to stay competitive in a rapidly changing market.

Given the conservative nature of pension funds, any significant change in investment strategy requires the approval of the board of trustees. The board comprises individuals responsible for overseeing the fund's management and ensuring it aligns with the long-term interests of the beneficiaries. The proposal to invest in cryptocurrencies is presented to the board with detailed research and analysis.

This proposal includes:

- A comprehensive overview of the cryptocurrency market.
- Potential benefits and risks associated with cryptocurrency investments.
- Case studies and performance data of other institutional investors who have ventured into this space.
- An assessment of the regulatory environment and its implications for institutional investors.
- A proposed allocation strategy, including the percentage of the portfolio to be invested in cryptocurrencies.

Once the board approves the initial proposal, the next step involves thorough due diligence and research. This phase is critical as it lays the groundwork for informed decision-making. Pension fund managers engage in extensive research to understand the cryptocurrency ecosystem, market dynamics, and technological underpinnings. They often collaborate with external experts, consultants, and research firms specializing in digital assets.

Key areas of focus during this phase include:

- Market Analysis: Understanding the historical performance, volatility, and liquidity of major cryptocurrencies like Bitcoin and Ethereum.

-

Regulatory Landscape: Evaluating the current regulatory environment and potential future developments that could impact cryptocurrency investments.

- Security and Custody Solutions: Identifying reputable custodians and secure storage solutions to mitigate the risk of theft or loss.

-Technological Infrastructure: Assessing the technology and infrastructure supporting cryptocurrency trading, including exchanges and trading platforms.

- Risk Management: Also key is developing a robust risk management framework to address the unique risks associated with cryptocurrencies.

One of the primary concerns for institutional investors is the safe custody of digital assets. Unlike traditional assets, cryptocurrencies require specialized storage solutions to protect against hacking and theft. Pension funds must select a reliable and secure custodian to store their digital assets.

Custodians offering institutional-grade services, such as Coinbase Custody, Fidelity Digital Assets, and BitGo, are evaluated based on several criteria:

- Security Measures:
The custodian's security protocols, including multi-signature wallets, cold storage solutions, and insurance coverage.

- Regulatory Compliance: Ensuring the custodian complies with relevant regulatory requirements and has a track record of transparency and reliability.

- Service Offerings: Additional services such as staking, lending, and reporting that can add value to the pension fund's investment strategy.

Developing an Investment Strategy

With the due diligence phase complete and a custodian selected, the next step involves developing a comprehensive investment strategy. This strategy outlines the approach the pension fund will take to invest in cryptocurrencies and manage these assets within their broader portfolio.

Key components of the investment strategy include:

Allocation Strategy: Determining the percentage of the portfolio to be allocated to cryptocurrencies. This allocation is typically small, ranging from 1% to 5%, to balance potential high returns with the inherent risks.

Diversification: Deciding whether to invest in a single cryptocurrency, such as Bitcoin, or diversify across multiple digital assets. Diversification can help mitigate risks associated with individual cryptocurrencies.

Entry and Exit Points: Establishing criteria for entering and exiting positions in the cryptocurrency market. This includes setting price targets, stop-loss levels, and rebalancing schedules.
Risk Management:

Implementing a risk management framework to monitor and mitigate risks. This includes regular portfolio reviews, stress testing, and scenario analysis.

Compliance and Reporting: Ensuring compliance with regulatory requirements and establishing robust reporting mechanisms to provide transparency to stakeholders.

Once the investment strategy is finalized, the next phase involves executing the strategy and implementing the plan. This phase requires careful coordination and precise execution to ensure a smooth transition.

Key steps in this phase include:

Account Setup: Opening accounts with selected cryptocurrency exchanges and custodians. This involves completing necessary documentation, KYC (Know Your Customer) procedures, and integrating with the custodian's infrastructure.

Initial Purchase: Making the initial purchase of cryptocurrencies based on the allocation strategy. This is typically done in stages to avoid significant market impact and ensure favorable entry points.

Secure Storage: Transferring purchased cryptocurrencies to the custodian's secure storage solutions. This involves using multi-signature wallets and cold storage to protect against theft and hacking.

Ongoing Management: Continuously monitoring the cryptocurrency portfolio and adjusting as needed. This includes rebalancing the portfolio, managing risks, and staying informed about market developments and regulatory changes.

Investing in cryptocurrencies requires a deep understanding of the market and technology. Pension funds invest in educating and training their investment teams to ensure they are well-equipped to manage digital assets effectively.

This education encompasses: Market Dynamics: Understanding the factors driving cryptocurrency prices, including macroeconomic trends, regulatory developments, and technological advancements.

Technical Aspects: Gaining knowledge about blockchain technology, consensus mechanisms, and the technical aspects of cryptocurrencies.

Risk Management: Learning about best practices in risk management and security protocols to safeguard digital assets.

Given the complexities of the cryptocurrency market, pension funds often engage external advisors and consultants with expertise in digital assets. These advisors provide valuable insights, assist with strategy development, and offer ongoing support to ensure successful implementation.

External advisors can help with:

Market Research: Providing in-depth research and analysis of the cryptocurrency market and identifying potential investment opportunities.

Regulatory Guidance: Offering guidance on navigating the regulatory landscape and ensuring compliance with relevant regulations.

Risk Management: Assisting in the development and implementation of robust risk management frameworks.

Continuous monitoring and reporting are crucial to managing cryptocurrency investments effectively. Pension funds establish robust monitoring and reporting mechanisms to track the performance of their cryptocurrency portfolio and provide transparency to stakeholders.

Key components of monitoring and reporting include:

Performance Tracking: Regularly monitoring the performance of cryptocurrency investments and comparing them against benchmarks and performance targets.

Risk Monitoring: Continuously assessing risks and implementing measures to mitigate potential threats.

This includes monitoring market volatility, regulatory changes, and security threats.

Reporting:
Providing regular reports to the board of trustees and other stakeholders, detailing the performance, risks, and overall status of the cryptocurrency portfolio.

Adapting to Market developments is dynamic and constantly evolving. Pension funds must stay agile and adapt to market developments to capitalize on opportunities and manage risks effectively.

This involves staying informed about:

Regulatory Changes: Keeping abreast of changes in the regulatory environment and adjusting strategies to remain compliant.

Technological Advancements: Staying updated on technological innovations and their potential impact on the cryptocurrency market.

Market Trends: Monitoring market trends and sentiment to identify potential investment opportunities and risks.

Communication with Beneficiaries

Transparency and communication with beneficiaries are critical components of managing a pension fund. When incorporating cryptocurrencies into the portfolio, it is essential to communicate the rationale, benefits, and risks to the beneficiaries. This helps build trust and ensures beneficiaries understand the strategic decisions being made on their behalf.

Communication strategies include:

Regular Updates: Providing regular updates through newsletters, reports, and meetings to keep beneficiaries informed about the performance and status of cryptocurrency investments.

Educational Sessions: Offering educational sessions and resources to help beneficiaries understand cryptocurrencies and their role in the investment strategy.

Addressing Concerns:

Addressing any concerns or questions from beneficiaries and providing clear explanations to build confidence in the investment strategy.

Expanding a pension fund's portfolio to include cryptocurrencies is a complex and multifaceted process that requires careful planning, due diligence, and strategic execution. By following a structured approach, pension funds can effectively navigate the challenges and capitalize on the opportunities presented by the rapidly evolving cryptocurrency market.

The process begins with recognizing the potential benefits and securing board approval, followed by extensive research and due diligence to understand the market and its risks. Selecting a reliable custodian and developing a comprehensive investment strategy are critical steps in ensuring the safe and effective management of digital assets.

Executing the investment strategy involves precise coordination and ongoing management, supported by continuous education, external advisors, and robust monitoring and reporting mechanisms. Staying agile and adapting to market developments, along with transparent communication with beneficiaries, further enhances the successful integration of cryptocurrencies into the pension fund's portfolio.

By taking a cautious yet proactive approach, pension funds can position themselves to benefit from the transformative potential of digital assets, enhance diversification, and achieve long-term growth and stability for their beneficiaries.

Popular Cryptocurrencies

While Bitcoin is the most well-known cryptocurrency, there are thousands of other cryptocurrencies, each with their own unique features and use cases. Here are a few of the most popular cryptocurrencies:

1. **Bitcoin (BTC): Often referred to as digital gold, Bitcoin was the first cryptocurrency and remains the largest by market

capitalization. It is used as a store of value and a medium of exchange.

2. Ethereum (ETH): Ethereum is a decentralized platform that enables smart contracts and decentralized applications (DApps) to be built and deployed without any downtime, fraud, control, or interference from a third party.

3. Ripple (XRP): Ripple is a digital payment protocol that enables fast, low-cost international money transfers. It aims to bridge the gap between traditional financial

systems and blockchain technology.

4. Litecoin (LTC): Created as a "lighter" version of Bitcoin, Litecoin offers faster transaction confirmation times and a different hashing algorithm.

5. Cardano (ADA): Cardano is a blockchain platform that aims to provide a more secure and scalable infrastructure for the development of decentralized applications and smart contracts.

Chapter 9: Why Institutions

Institutional investors, including hedge funds, asset managers, and family offices, have begun allocating capital to cryptocurrencies, seeking diversification, alpha generation, and exposure to transformative technologies. With the backing of institutional capital, the cryptocurrency market has experienced unprecedented growth and legitimacy. Several publicly traded companies, such as Tesla, MicroStrategy, and Square, have added Bitcoin to their corporate treasuries as a hedge against inflation and currency devaluation. These companies view Bitcoin as a store of value and a strategic asset that can preserve purchasing power in an uncertain economic environment.

The rise of decentralized finance (DeFi) is transforming the landscape of the financial industry, offering new opportunities and challenges for institutional investors. As pension funds, asset managers, and other institutional entities seek to diversify their portfolios and enhance returns, they are increasingly exploring the DeFi space. This narrative delves into how institutional investors are leveraging DeFi to expand their portfolios, focusing on the processes, strategies, and considerations involved in this burgeoning sector.

Decentralized finance, commonly known as DeFi, refers to a suite of financial services built on blockchain technology, primarily Ethereum. Unlike traditional financial systems that rely on intermediaries such as banks and brokers, DeFi leverages smart contracts to automate and decentralize financial transactions. These smart contracts are self-executing agreements with the terms of the contract directly written into code, enabling trustless and transparent financial interactions.

DeFi encompasses a wide range of applications, including lending and borrowing platforms, decentralized exchanges (DEXs), stablecoins, yield farming, and synthetic assets. These innovations offer various financial services without the need for centralized intermediaries, making them highly attractive for both individual and institutional investors.

Institutional investors are drawn to the DeFi space for several reasons:

1. High Yield Opportunities: DeFi platforms often offer significantly higher yields compared to traditional financial instruments. For example, yield farming and liquidity provision can generate returns far exceeding those of traditional savings accounts or bonds.

2. Diversification:

DeFi represents a new asset class with unique characteristics and risk-return profiles. Including DeFi assets in a portfolio can enhance diversification and reduce overall risk.

3. Efficiency and Innovation: DeFi platforms operate 24/7 without geographical limitations, providing greater flexibility and efficiency in financial operations. The rapid pace of innovation in DeFi also presents opportunities for first movers to capitalize on new financial products and services.

4. Transparency and Accessibility: Blockchain technology ensures transparency in transactions, reducing the risk of fraud and improving trust. Additionally, DeFi platforms are accessible to anyone with an internet connection, democratizing access to financial services.

Before diving into the DeFi space, institutional investors should conduct thorough research and due diligence. This involves understanding the fundamental principles of DeFi, the underlying technologies, and the specific risks associated with decentralized platforms.

Key areas of research include:

Market Analysis: Examining the growth trends, total value locked (TVL), and the performance of various DeFi protocols.

Platform Evaluation: Assessing the most prominent DeFi platforms such as Aave, Compound, Uniswap, MakerDAO, and their respective use cases.

Risk Assessment:

Identifying potential risks, including smart contract vulnerabilities, regulatory uncertainties, and market volatility.

Regulatory Landscape: Understanding the current and evolving regulatory environment for DeFi and how it impacts institutional participation.

Once the initial research phase is complete, institutional investors develop a comprehensive DeFi strategy. This strategy outlines how they plan to incorporate

DeFi into their portfolios and manage the associated risks.

Key components of a DeFi strategy include:

1. Allocation Strategy: Determining the percentage of the portfolio to be allocated to DeFi assets. Given the high-risk nature of DeFi, institutions typically start with a small allocation, gradually increasing it as they gain confidence and experience.

2. Platform Selection: Choosing which DeFi platforms to invest in based

on factors such as security, liquidity, user base, and historical performance. Institutions often diversify across multiple platforms to mitigate risk.

3. Yield Farming and Liquidity Provision: Identifying opportunities for yield farming and providing liquidity to decentralized exchanges. These activities involve supplying assets to DeFi protocols in exchange for rewards, which can be significantly higher than traditional fixed-income investments.

4. Stablecoins: Utilizing stablecoins, which are pegged to fiat currencies, to minimize volatility and facilitate transactions within the DeFi ecosystem. Stablecoins such as USDC, DAI, and USDT play a crucial role in DeFi strategies.

5. Risk Management: Implementing robust risk management practices, including regular audits of smart contracts, diversification of assets, and continuous monitoring of platform security and performance.

With a strategy in place, institutional investors move to the execution phase, which involves the actual deployment of capital into DeFi platforms. This phase requires meticulous planning and coordination to ensure a smooth transition.

Account Setup and Security Measures:

Institutions begin by setting up accounts on selected DeFi platforms and ensuring that robust security measures are in place. This includes using hardware wallets, multi-signature accounts, and secure custody solutions to protect digital assets.

Initial investments are made cautiously, often in stages, to minimize market impact and manage risk. Institutions may start by providing liquidity to decentralized exchanges or participating in lending protocols to earn interest on their assets. Once investments are made, continuous monitoring is crucial to manage risk and optimize returns. This involves tracking the performance of DeFi assets, monitoring market conditions, and staying informed about any updates or changes to the protocols being used. Active participation in the DeFi ecosystem is essential for institutional investors to stay ahead of the curve. This involves engaging with DeFi communities, developers, and other stakeholders to gain insights and contribute to the growth and development of the ecosystem.

Many DeFi platforms are governed by decentralized autonomous organizations (DAOs) where token holders can vote on key decisions. Institutional investors, as significant stakeholders, can participate in governance to influence the direction and policies of these platforms. Forming collaborations and partnerships with DeFi projects and other institutional players can provide strategic advantages. This can include initiatives or projects, participating in joint research initiatives, or providing liquidity in a coordinated manner.

The DeFi space is not without its risks and challenges. Institutional investors must be proactive in managing these to safeguard their investments. For starters, smart contract vulnerabilities are a significant risk in DeFi. Institutions mitigate this by investing in projects with audited and tested contracts, and by diversifying across multiple protocols to spread risk. Another challenge is the cryptocurrency market, known for its volatility, which can impact the value of DeFi investments. Institutions manage this by maintaining a diversified portfolio and using stablecoins to hedge against price fluctuations.

Regulatory uncertainties are a major concern in the DeFi space. Institutions should stay informed about regulatory developments and engage with regulators to ensure compliance and advocate for favorable regulations. A major risk factor is called operational risks, which includes the potential for platform failures or hacks, and can be mitigated through thorough due diligence, continuous monitoring, and the use of secure custody solutions.

Several high-profile institutional investors have successfully ventured into the DeFi space, providing valuable case studies for others to follow.

Case Study 1: Andreessen Horowitz (a16z): Andreessen Horowitz, a leading venture capital firm, has been a prominent investor in the DeFi space. The firm's Crypto Fund has invested in various DeFi projects, including Compound, MakerDAO, and Uniswap. a16z's involvement goes beyond financial investment; they actively participate in governance and provide strategic support to the projects they invest in.

Case Study 2: Polychain Capital:
Polychain Capital, a cryptocurrency investment firm, has a significant portion of its portfolio allocated to DeFi assets. The firm invests in DeFi protocols and participates in yield farming and liquidity provision to generate returns. Polychain's strategic approach and early investments in successful DeFi projects have yielded substantial returns.

Case Study 3: Galaxy Digital:
Galaxy Digital, a diversified financial services firm focused on digital assets, has been an

active participant in the DeFi space. The firm provides liquidity to decentralized exchanges, invests in DeFi startups, and leverages its extensive network to support the growth of the DeFi ecosystem. Galaxy Digital's involvement demonstrates how traditional financial firms can effectively integrate DeFi into their operations.

The Future of Institutional Investment in DeFi

The involvement of institutional investors in the DeFi space is still in its early stages, but the potential for growth is immense. As the DeFi ecosystem continues to mature and address existing challenges, institutional participation is expected to increase significantly. The rapid pace of innovation in DeFi will continue to create new opportunities for institutional investors. Emerging trends such as decentralized insurance, cross-chain interoperability, and tokenized real-world assets will expand the scope of DeFi and attract more institutional capital. As security measures and regulatory frameworks improve, institutional investors will feel more confident about investing in DeFi. Enhanced security protocols, regular audits, and compliance with regulatory standards will mitigate risks and facilitate broader adoption.

The integration of DeFi with traditional finance (TradFi) will create synergies and new financial products. Institutions that bridge the gap between DeFi and TradFi can offer innovative solutions that leverage the strengths of both systems. The success of early adopters has inspired more institutional investors to explore DeFi. As more pension funds, asset managers, and other institutions recognize the benefits of DeFi, the flow of institutional capital into the space will accelerate.

The journey of institutional investors into the DeFi space is marked by careful planning, strategic execution, and proactive risk management. By leveraging the unique opportunities presented by DeFi, institutions can enhance portfolio diversification, achieve higher returns, and stay at the forefront of financial innovation. The process begins with thorough research and due diligence, followed by the development of a robust DeFi strategy. Execution involves cautious deployment of capital, continuous monitoring, and active engagement with the DeFi ecosystem. Managing risks and staying informed about regulatory developments are crucial to safeguarding investments and ensuring long-term success. As the DeFi space continues to evolve, institutional investors will play a crucial role in its maturation and mainstream adoption. Their involvement brings not only substantial capital but also a level of professionalism, scrutiny, and advocacy that can help address many of the current challenges facing the DeFi sector.

Collaboration with DeFi Developers:

Institutional investors have begun to recognize the importance of contributing to the ecosystem beyond mere capital infusion. By collaborating closely with DeFi developers and projects, these investors can influence the development of features that align with institutional needs, such as enhanced security protocols, better user interfaces, and comprehensive compliance tools. These collaborations can take the form of direct partnerships, advisory roles, or funding development grants. Active participation in governance is another critical aspect. By holding governance tokens, institutional investors can vote on important protocol changes, fee structures, and development roadmaps. This active involvement ensures that the DeFi platforms evolve in ways that are conducive to large-scale investment and operational security.

Institutional involvement necessitates rigorous security measures. Many DeFi projects now conduct regular audits and security assessments to reassure investors about the robustness of their protocols. Institutions often require these audits before committing significant funds. Some have even started engaging third-party cybersecurity firms to conduct independent reviews of the smart contracts and platform architecture.

The rise of decentralized insurance protocols is another development catering to institutional needs. Platforms like Nexus Mutual and Cover Protocol offer insurance against smart contract failures and hacks. Institutional investors leverage these insurance products to protect their DeFi investments, adding an additional layer of risk mitigation.

As mentioned, several times throughout the previous pages, the regulatory environment for cryptocurrencies and DeFi continues to evolve. Institutions are leading the charge in advocating for clear, favorable regulatory frameworks. They work closely with regulators to ensure that new regulations protect investors without stifling innovation. Institutions also invest in compliance tools and services that help navigate the regulatory landscape, ensuring that their operations remain within legal boundaries.

To that end, algorithmic trading and arbitrage strategies are being increasingly employed in the DeFi space. Institutions utilize sophisticated algorithms to take advantage of price discrepancies between different DeFi platforms and traditional exchanges. This approach not only generates additional returns but also contributes to market efficiency and liquidity. Many DeFi protocols offer staking rewards and governance tokens as incentives.

Institutional investors are exploring these opportunities to earn passive income and gain a say in protocol governance. By staking assets, institutions can earn rewards while supporting the network's security and operations.

Secure custody solutions are paramount for institutional involvement in DeFi. Institutions rely on advanced custody solutions that offer features like multi-signature wallets, hardware security modules, and insurance against loss. Providers such as Anchorage, BitGo, and Fireblocks cater specifically to institutional needs, ensuring the safekeeping of digital assets.

To manage DeFi investments effectively, institutions invest in training programs for their staff. These programs cover the technical aspects of blockchain technology, the specifics of various DeFi protocols, and the nuances of managing digital assets. Continuous education ensures that investment teams are up to date with the latest developments and best practices.

Institutions are also at the forefront of establishing industry standards and best practices for DeFi investments. These standards cover areas such as security, transparency, and operational efficiency. By adhering to these standards, institutions can foster trust and reliability within the DeFi ecosystem.

One of the most significant future trends is the integration of DeFi with traditional financial services. Hybrid models are emerging where traditional financial institutions incorporate DeFi protocols into their service offerings, providing clients with innovative financial products that leverage the benefits of both systems. This hybrid model led to the tokenization of real-world assets, such as real estate, commodities, and equities, and represents a promising area for institutional investment. DeFi platforms facilitating this tokenization allow for fractional ownership, increased liquidity, and broader market access. Institutions are beginning to explore these opportunities to further diversify their portfolios and tap into new markets.

One such market is Cross-chain interoperability, which enables different blockchain networks to communicate and transact with each other. This model is used to revolutionize the DeFi space. Protocols like Polkadot, Cosmos, and

Chainlink are at the forefront of this development. Institutional investors are keenly watching these advancements, as interoperability can significantly enhance liquidity and open new investment opportunities across various blockchain ecosystems.

Privacy is also a growing concern for institutional investors. Enhanced privacy solutions, such as zero-knowledge proofs and privacy-focused DeFi protocols, are being developed to protect transaction data and ensure confidentiality. Institutions are likely to adopt these solutions to safeguard sensitive financial information.

Sustainable and ethical investments are gaining traction within the DeFi space. Projects that focus on environmental sustainability, social impact, and ethical governance are attracting institutional interest. By investing in these projects, institutions can align their portfolios with their values and meet the growing demand for socially responsible investments.

Because of the strategies mentioned, Institutional investors are progressively exploring and integrating DeFi into their portfolios, driven by the promise of high yields, diversification, and the innovative potential of blockchain technology. The process begins with thorough research and strategic planning, followed by careful execution and ongoing risk management. As institutions engage more deeply with the DeFi ecosystem, they contribute to its maturation, security, and mainstream adoption.

By adopting advanced security measures, participating in governance, and leveraging innovative financial products, institutions can capitalize on the opportunities presented by DeFi while managing the associated risks. The involvement of institutional capital not only brings legitimacy to the DeFi space but also drives further innovation and development.

As DeFi continues to evolve, the integration with traditional financial services, the tokenization of real-world assets, cross-chain interoperability, and enhanced privacy solutions will shape the future of decentralized finance. Institutional investors who navigate this landscape effectively will be well-positioned to reap the benefits of this transformative financial revolution.

In summary, the journey of institutional investors into the DeFi space is a complex and multifaceted process that requires careful planning, strategic execution, and proactive risk management. By leveraging the unique opportunities presented by DeFi, institutions can enhance portfolio diversification, achieve higher returns, and stay at the forefront of financial innovation. As the DeFi ecosystem continues to evolve, institutional investors will play a crucial role in its maturation and mainstream adoption, driving the next wave of financial innovation and growth.

In closing this chapter one thing hasn't been mentioned and that is Institutional Investors are most interested in scalability. Scalability remains a pressing issue for blockchain networks, with concerns about transaction throughput, latency, and energy consumption. As adoption grows, blockchain platforms must find scalable solutions that balance performance, security, and decentralization while minimizing environmental impact. Regulatory uncertainty poses a significant challenge for cryptocurrency adoption and innovation, with divergent approaches and conflicting regulations across jurisdictions. Clear and consistent regulatory frameworks are essential to foster trust, protect investors, and promote responsible innovation in the crypto industry.

As we reflect on the journey through the crypto landscape, one thing is clear: the future of cryptocurrency is full of promise and possibility. From its humble beginnings as an obscure digital experiment to its status as a global phenomenon, cryptocurrency has come a long way in a relatively short time.

While navigating the challenges and opportunities ahead, let us remember the principles that underpin the crypto movement: decentralization, transparency, and empowerment. By staying true to these values and embracing innovation, we can build a more inclusive, equitable, and resilient financial system for the future.

Chapter 10: The Next Frontier

As we stand on the cusp of a new era in finance, the future of cryptocurrency beckons with boundless potential and unprecedented possibilities. In this chapter, we'll embark on a journey into the unknown, exploring the innovations, trends, and challenges that will shape the evolution of cryptocurrency in the years to come.

Decentralized Finance (DeFi)

As mentioned in the previous chapter decentralized finance

(DeFi) has emerged as one of the most exciting and disruptive trends in the cryptocurrency space, offering a vision of a more open, transparent, and inclusive financial system. From decentralized lending and borrowing to automated market-making and yield farming, DeFi projects are reimagining traditional financial services on the blockchain.

DeFi protocols, built on blockchain platforms like Ethereum, enable peer-to-peer lending, decentralized exchanges, and other financial services without the need for intermediaries. Projects like Compound, Aave, and MakerDAO have pioneered innovative DeFi applications, unlocking new opportunities for users to earn, borrow, and trade digital assets.

Automated market makers (AMMs) are at the heart of decentralized exchanges (DEXs), facilitating peer-to-peer trading and liquidity provision without the need for order books or centralized intermediaries. Protocols like Uniswap, SushiSwap, and PancakeSwap use AMMs to enable seamless and permissionless trading of a wide range of digital assets.

Non-fungible tokens (NFTs) have taken the world by storm, offering a new way to buy, sell, and own digital assets with unique properties and characteristics. From digital art and collectibles to virtual real estate and in-game items, NFTs are revolutionizing the concept of ownership and value in the digital age.

NFT marketplaces like OpenSea, Rarible, and Foundation provide platforms for creators and collectors to buy, sell, and trade NFTs with ease. These marketplaces offer a diverse range of digital assets, from digital art and music to virtual real estate and domain names, attracting a global audience of creators and collectors.

NFTs have applications beyond the art world, with potential use cases in gaming, virtual reality, entertainment, and more. Projects like Decentraland, CryptoPunks, and NBA Top Shot are exploring the possibilities of NFTs in virtual worlds, digital collectibles, and immersive experiences, blurring the lines between the physical and digital realms.

Blockchain technology continues to evolve and innovate, with new consensus mechanisms, scalability solutions, and privacy features paving the way for the next generation of blockchain platforms and applications. From Proof of Stake (PoS) to sharding and layer 2 solutions, developers are exploring novel approaches to address the scalability, security, and usability challenges of blockchain networks.

Proof of Stake (PoS) consensus mechanisms, such as Ethereum 2.0's Beacon Chain, aim to improve the energy efficiency and scalability of blockchain networks by replacing energy-intensive mining with staking. PoS networks rely on validators to secure the network and validate transactions, reducing the environmental impact of blockchain operations. Layer 2 scaling solutions, like the Lightning Network for Bitcoin and Optimistic Rollups for Ethereum, aim to increase transaction throughput and reduce fees by processing transactions off-chain and settling them on the main blockchain periodically. These solutions enable faster and cheaper transactions while maintaining the security and decentralization of the underlying blockchain.

As cryptocurrency adoption grows, regulators around the world are grappling with how to regulate this rapidly evolving industry. From anti-money laundering (AML) and know-your-customer (KYC) requirements to securities laws and tax compliance, navigating the regulatory landscape poses challenges for businesses, investors, and developers in the crypto space. Regulatory clarity is essential for the long-term success and mainstream adoption of cryptocurrency and blockchain technology. Governments and regulatory bodies need to provide clear guidelines and frameworks that strike a balance between innovation and investor protection, fostering trust and confidence in the industry.

Compliance tools and solutions, such as blockchain analytics, identity verification, and transaction monitoring, help businesses and financial institutions comply with regulatory requirements and mitigate the risk of fraud, money laundering, and other illicit activities. By implementing robust compliance measures, companies can build trust with regulators and stakeholders while safeguarding the integrity of the crypto ecosystem.

The Role of Institutional Investors and Corporate Adoption

Institutional investors and corporations play a crucial

role in driving the adoption and mainstream acceptance of cryptocurrency. From hedge funds and asset managers to Fortune 500 companies, institutional players bring credibility, capital, and expertise to the crypto space, shaping its growth and evolution. These institutional investors employ a variety of investment strategies when entering the crypto space, from long-term buy-and-hold approaches to active trading strategies and opportunistic investments. The institutions contribute to market liquidity, stability, and maturation, paving the way for broader institutional adoption and acceptance. This has led to corporate adoption of cryptocurrency and blockchain technology and placed it with companies exploring ways to leverage digital assets for payments, remittances, supply chain management, and more. From accepting Bitcoin as payment to building blockchain-based solutions, corporations are embracing innovation and disruption in the digital age.

As we look to the future of cryptocurrency, one thing is clear: the possibilities are endless. From decentralized

finance and non-fungible
tokens to blockchain
technology and institutional
adoption, cryptocurrency is
reshaping the way we think
about money, value, and
ownership in the digital age.
By embracing innovation,
collaboration, and responsible
stewardship, we can harness
the power of cryptocurrency
to create a more equitable,
transparent, and inclusive
financial system for all. As we
navigate the challenges and
opportunities ahead, let us
chart a course towards a
brighter future, where
cryptocurrency empowers
individuals, businesses, and

communities to thrive in the digital economy.

Chapter 11: The Revolution

A Call to Action

As we conclude our journey through the world of cryptocurrency, we are reminded of the incredible potential and transformative power of this revolutionary technology. In this final chapter, we issue a call to action for individuals, businesses, and policymakers to embrace the cryptocurrency revolution and seize the opportunities it presents for innovation, inclusion, and empowerment.

Cryptocurrency holds the promise of a more equitable, transparent, and accessible financial system, free from the limitations and inequalities of traditional banking and finance. By leveraging blockchain technology, cryptocurrencies offer solutions to longstanding challenges such as financial exclusion, censorship, and lack of transparency, empowering individuals to take control of their finances and participate in the global economy.

Cryptocurrency has the potential to bridge the gap

between the banked and unbanked populations, providing access to financial services for millions of people around the world who are underserved or excluded by traditional banking systems. With a smartphone and an internet connection, anyone can participate in the cryptocurrency economy, send, and receive money, access credit and savings, and build wealth for the future.

Blockchain technology enables transparent and immutable record-keeping, ensuring the integrity and traceability of financial transactions on a decentralized ledger. By leveraging the transparency of the blockchain, cryptocurrencies promote accountability and trust in financial transactions, reducing the risk of fraud, corruption, and mismanagement.

Cryptocurrency is a hotbed of innovation and disruption, driving advances in blockchain technology, decentralized finance (DeFi), non-fungible tokens (NFTs), and beyond. From peer-to-peer lending and decentralized exchanges to digital art and virtual real estate, the possibilities for innovation are limitless in crypto space, pushing the boundaries of what is possible in finance, technology, and beyond. To fully realize the potential of cryptocurrency, we must seize the opportunities it presents and embrace the principles of innovation, collaboration, and responsible stewardship. Whether you're an individual investor, a business leader, or a policymaker, there are steps you can take to contribute to the cryptocurrency revolution and shape its future trajectory.

For Individuals you can participate in the cryptocurrency revolution by educating yourself about blockchain technology and digital assets, investing responsibly in cryptocurrencies, and advocating for regulatory clarity and consumer protection. By staying informed and engaged, you can make informed decisions about your financial future and help drive the adoption and acceptance of cryptocurrency in society.

Businesses can leverage cryptocurrency to streamline

operations, reduce costs, and unlock new revenue streams. By accepting cryptocurrency payments, implementing blockchain-based solutions, and exploring partnerships with blockchain projects, businesses can gain a competitive edge in the digital economy and tap into new markets and opportunities. Additionally, businesses can prioritize sustainability and social responsibility by adopting environmentally friendly blockchain technologies and supporting initiatives that promote financial inclusion and empowerment.

Policymakers play a crucial role in shaping the regulatory landscape for cryptocurrency and blockchain technology. By engaging with industry stakeholders, conducting research, and crafting clear and balanced regulatory frameworks, policymakers can foster innovation, protect consumers, and promote economic growth and stability. Additionally, policymakers can invest in education and infrastructure to support the development and adoption of cryptocurrency and blockchain technology.

While cryptocurrency holds immense promise, it also faces significant challenges and barriers to adoption. From regulatory uncertainty and scalability issues to security concerns and environmental impact, the crypto industry must address these challenges head-on to realize its full potential and gain widespread acceptance in society.

To recap, regulatory clarity is essential for the long-term success and mainstream adoption of cryptocurrency. Policymakers must work collaboratively with industry stakeholders to develop clear and balanced regulatory frameworks that protect consumers, foster innovation, and promote financial inclusion while mitigating the risks associated with digital assets.

The lack of regulatory clarity means scalability remains a pressing issue for blockchain networks, with concerns about transaction throughput, latency, and energy consumption. The crypto industry must invest in research and development to address scalability challenges and explore sustainable solutions that balance performance, security, and environmental impact.

Security and privacy are also paramount in the crypto space, with hackers and malicious actors constantly seeking to exploit vulnerabilities and steal funds. The industry must prioritize security best practices, implement robust cybersecurity measures, and educate users about the importance of protecting their digital assets to safeguard against threats and ensure the integrity of the crypto ecosystem.

As we conclude our exploration of the cryptocurrency revolution, we are reminded of the incredible journey we have embarked upon and the endless possibilities that lie ahead. By embracing innovation, collaboration, and responsible stewardship, we can harness the power of cryptocurrency to build a more inclusive, transparent, and resilient financial system for all.

Together, let us seize the opportunities presented by cryptocurrency to create a brighter future for generations to come. Whether you're an individual investor, a business leader, or a policymaker, now is the time to act and be part of the cryptocurrency revolution. The future is ours to shape, and the possibilities are limitless.

Bonus Recap:

Institutional Investing in Crypto vs. Traditional Strategies: Unleashing the Power of Digital Assets

Institutional investors, including hedge funds, asset managers, pension funds, and family offices, face a critical decision when it comes to allocating capital: whether to embrace the emerging asset class of cryptocurrency or stick to traditional investment strategies. In this bonus chapter, we'll explore the benefits and advantages that institutional investors can gain by investing in crypto compared to those who choose to stay the course with traditional investment approaches.

Cryptocurrency, once considered a niche asset class, has emerged as a viable investment option for institutional investors seeking diversification, alpha generation, and exposure to transformative technologies. Here are some compelling reasons why institutional investors should consider adding crypto to their investment portfolios:

Potential for High Returns

Cryptocurrency markets have demonstrated the potential for significant returns over the past decade, with assets like Bitcoin and Ethereum delivering outsized gains compared to traditional asset classes. Institutional investors who allocate a portion of their portfolio to crypto assets may benefit from exposure to high-growth opportunities and alpha generation potential.

Diversification Benefits

Cryptocurrency offers diversification benefits for institutional portfolios, as digital assets have historically exhibited low correlation with traditional asset classes like stocks, bonds, and commodities. By adding crypto to their investment mix, institutional investors can reduce overall portfolio risk and enhance risk-adjusted returns through diversification.

Hedge Against Inflation

In an environment of rising inflation and currency devaluation, cryptocurrency serves as a hedge against the erosion of purchasing power. Assets like Bitcoin, with a capped supply and deflationary monetary policy, offer protection against fiat currency debasement and macroeconomic uncertainty, making them attractive stores of value for institutional investors seeking inflation protection.

Exposure to Innovation and Technology

Cryptocurrency and blockchain technology represent a paradigm shift in finance and technology, offering disruptive solutions to traditional financial services and enabling new business models and use cases. By investing in crypto assets, institutional investors gain exposure to innovative technologies and digital ecosystems that have the potential to reshape industries and create new value propositions.

Liquidity and Market Access

Cryptocurrency markets offer high liquidity and round-the-clock trading, providing institutional investors with ample opportunities to enter and exit positions efficiently. With the proliferation of cryptocurrency exchanges, trading platforms, and liquidity providers, institutional investors can access crypto markets with ease and flexibility, enhancing portfolio liquidity and execution efficiency.

Portfolio Customization and Tailored Strategies

Cryptocurrency allows institutional investors to customize their investment strategies and tailor their portfolios to meet specific risk and return objectives. Whether through direct investment in digital assets, participation in decentralized finance (DeFi) protocols, or exposure to blockchain-based venture capital opportunities, institutional investors can design bespoke strategies that align with their investment mandates and preferences.

Sticking to Traditional Strategies: The Case for Caution

While cryptocurrency offers compelling benefits for institutional investors, there are also risks and challenges associated with investing in this nascent asset class. Here are some considerations for institutional investors who choose to stick to traditional investment strategies:

Regulatory Uncertainty

Cryptocurrency markets operate in a rapidly evolving regulatory landscape, with governments and regulatory bodies around the world grappling with how to classify and regulate digital assets. Institutional investors may face regulatory uncertainty and compliance risks when investing in crypto, as regulations vary by jurisdiction and can impact market access, liquidity, and investor protection.

Volatility and Risk

Cryptocurrency markets are known for their high volatility and price fluctuations, with assets like Bitcoin experiencing rapid price swings over short periods. Institutional investors with low risk tolerance or strict risk management policies may view crypto's volatility as a deterrent and prefer the stability of traditional asset classes like stocks and bonds.

Security and Custody Concerns

Security and custody are paramount in the crypto space, as digital assets are vulnerable to hacking, theft, and loss if not stored and managed securely. Institutional investors may have concerns about the security and reliability of cryptocurrency custody solutions, especially given the lack of regulatory oversight and the prevalence of cybersecurity threats in the crypto ecosystem.

Market Manipulation and Fraud

Cryptocurrency markets are susceptible to manipulation and fraudulent activities, including pump-and-dump schemes, wash trading, and insider trading. Institutional investors may be wary of investing in crypto assets due to concerns about market manipulation, lack of transparency, and the presence of bad actors in the industry.

Lack of Institutional Infrastructure

Despite the growing interest from institutional investors, the cryptocurrency industry still lacks mature infrastructure and institutional-grade services compared to traditional financial markets. Institutional investors may encounter challenges related to liquidity, market depth, and counterparty risk when navigating the crypto ecosystem, limiting their ability to deploy capital at scale.

Reputation and Stigma

Cryptocurrency remains a polarizing asset class, with lingering skepticism and stigma from mainstream investors, regulators, and the public. Institutional investors may face reputational risks and backlash from stakeholders if they allocate capital to crypto assets, especially if their investment decisions are perceived as speculative or risky.

Conclusion: Navigating the Path Forward

Institutional investors stand at a crossroads, facing a pivotal decision about whether to embrace the emerging asset class of cryptocurrency or adhere to traditional investment strategies. While both approaches have their merits and considerations, the rapid evolution and maturation of the crypto industry present compelling opportunities for institutional investors willing to venture into this new frontier.

For those institutions willing to embrace cryptocurrency, the potential benefits are significant: high returns, diversification, inflation protection, exposure to innovation, liquidity, and portfolio customization. By allocating a portion of their portfolios to crypto assets, institutional investors can position themselves to capitalize on the transformative potential of blockchain technology and digital assets, while mitigating risk and enhancing long-term performance.

However, it's essential for institutional investors to approach crypto investing with caution and diligence. Regulatory compliance, risk management, security, and due diligence are critical considerations when navigating the crypto landscape. By partnering with reputable service providers, conducting thorough research, and staying informed about regulatory developments, institutional investors can mitigate risks and maximize opportunities in the crypto space.

For those institutions opting to stick to traditional investment strategies, it's crucial to recognize the potential drawbacks and limitations of ignoring cryptocurrency. While traditional asset classes like stocks and bonds offer stability and familiarity, they may not provide the same level of growth and diversification opportunities as crypto assets. Moreover, as cryptocurrency continues to gain mainstream acceptance and adoption, institutions risk falling behind competitors and missing out on the potential upside of this emerging asset class.

Ultimately, the decision to invest in cryptocurrency or stick to traditional strategies will depend on each institution's risk tolerance, investment objectives, and long-term vision. However, it's essential for institutional investors to remain open-minded, adaptable, and forward-thinking in their approach to portfolio management. By embracing innovation, exploring new opportunities, and staying ahead of the curve, institutional investors can position themselves for success in the ever-changing landscape of global finance.

In conclusion, the cryptocurrency revolution represents a paradigm shift in finance, offering institutional investors unprecedented opportunities for growth, diversification, and innovation. Whether they choose to embrace crypto or stick to traditional strategies, institutional investors must carefully weigh the risks and rewards of each approach and chart a course that aligns with their goals and values. As the crypto industry continues to evolve and mature, one thing is clear: the future of finance is digital, and institutional investors have a crucial role to play in shaping it.